Online Multiplayer Games

Online Multiplayer Games

William Sims Bainbridge

ISBN: 978-3-031-01140-5   paperback
ISBN: 978-3-031-02268-5   ebook

DOI 10.1007/978-3-031-02268-5

A Publication in the Springer series
SYNTHESIS LECTURES ON INFORMATION CONCEPTS, RETRIEVAL, AND SERVICES

Lecture #13
Series Editor: Gary Marchionini, *University North Carolina, Chapel Hill*
Series ISSN
Synthesis Lectures on Information Concepts, Retrieval, and Services
Print 1947-945X   Electronic 1947-9468

Synthesis Lectures on Information Concepts, Retrieval, and Services

Editor
Gary Marchionini, *University North Carolina, Chapel Hill*

Online Multiplayer Games
William Sims Bainbridge
2010

Information Architecture: The Design and Integration of Information Spaces
Wei Ding, Xia Lin
2009

Reading and Writing the Electronic Book
Catherine C. Marshall
2009

Hypermedia Genes: An Evolutionary Perspective on Concepts, Models, and Architectures
Nuno M. Guimarães, Luís M. Carriço
2009

Understanding User-Web Interactions via Web Analytics
Bernard J. (Jim) Jansen
2009

XML Retrieval
Mounia Lalmas
2009

Faceted Search
Daniel Tunkelang
2009

Introduction to Webometrics: Quantitative Web Research for the Social Sciences
Michael Thelwall
2009

Exploratory Search: Beyond the Query-Response Paradigm
Ryen W. White, Resa A. Roth
2009

New Concepts in Digital Reference
R. David Lankes
2009

Automated Metadata in Multimedia Information Systems: Creation, Refinement, Use in Surrogates, and Evaluation
Michael G. Christel
2009

Online Multiplayer Games

William Sims Bainbridge

SYNTHESIS LECTURES ON INFORMATION CONCEPTS, RETRIEVAL, AND SERVICES #13

ABSTRACT

This lecture introduces fundamental principles of online multiplayer games, primarily massively multiplayer online role-playing games (MMORPGs), suitable for students and faculty interested both in designing games and in doing research on them. The general focus is human-centered computing, which includes many human-computer interaction issues and emphasizes social computing, but also, looks at how the design of socio-economic interactions extends our traditional notions of computer programming to cover human beings as well as machines. In addition, it demonstrates a range of social science research methodologies, both quantitative and qualitative, that could be used by students for term papers, or by their professors for publications. In addition to drawing upon a rich literature about these games, this lecture is based on thousands of hours of first-hand research experience inside many classic examples, including *World of Warcraft*, *The Matrix Online*, *Anarchy Online*, *Tabula Rasa*, *Entropia Universe*, *Dark Age of Camelot*, *Age of Conan*, *Lord of the Rings Online*, *Tale in the Desert*, *EVE Online*, *Star Wars Galaxies*, *Pirates of the Burning Sea*, and the non-game virtual world *Second Life*. Among the topics covered are historical-cultural origins of leading games, technical constraints that shape the experience, rolecoding and social control, player personality and motivation, relationships with avatars and characters, virtual professions and economies, social relations inside games, and the implications for the external society.

KEYWORDS

online game, MMORPG, virtual world, roleplaying game, human-centered computing, social computing

Contents

1   Introduction 1

    1.1   Types of Online Multiplayer Games 1

    1.2   Preserving Game History 4

    1.3   Intellectual Approaches to Games 5

    1.4   Research Topic Areas 9

2   Historical-Cultural Origins 11

    2.1   *A Tale in the Desert* 11

    2.2   *Dark Age of Camelot* 13

    2.3   *Age of Conan* 17

    2.4   *Lord of the Rings Online* 18

    2.5   *Star Wars Galaxies* 20

3   Technical Constraints 23

    3.1   Latency 23

    3.2   Sharding 26

    3.3   Graphics 28

4   Rolecoding and Social Control 35

    4.1   Systems of Rules 36

    4.2   Deviant Behavior 38

    4.3   Game Masters and Mentors 41

    4.4   Legal Regime 44

5   Personality and Motivation 47

    5.1   Psychological Theories and Typologies 47

    5.2   Game-Based Theories 48

	5.3	Theoretical Debates	51
	5.4	Non-Player Character Personality	54
6		Avatars and Characters	55
	6.1	Building a Bond with an Avatar	55
	6.2	The Quality of Avatar Relationships	58
	6.3	Secondary Avatars	60
	6.4	Facing the End	63
7		Virtual Professions and Economies	65
	7.1	Work in *Star Wars Galaxies*	65
	7.2	Production in *World of Warcraft*	68
	7.3	Division of Labor in Professions	70
8		Social Relations Inside Games	75
	8.1	Emergent Social Organization	75
	8.2	Examples of Guilds	77
	8.3	Quantitative Research on Guilds	79
9		Implications for External Society	81
	9.1	The Online Game Penumbra	81
	9.2	What People Learn in Online Games	83
	9.3	Research Opportunities	87
		Bibliography	91
		Author's Biography	105

CHAPTER 1

Introduction

This lecture will emphasize the dominant genre of online games, so-called *Massively-Multiplayer On-line Games* or MMORPGs, of which *World of Warcraft* is the most familiar example (Bainbridge, W., 2010b,c; Nardi, B., 2010). Although the boundaries of the concept are vague, the core idea is a some-what realistic computer-generated world in which the user is represented by an avatar or character, interacting with other characters, under the constraints of rules and to achieve goals set by the MMORPG's creators and by the players. The truth is, these are far more than mere games, because they provide virtual environments where people may socialize, explore, and to varying degrees, create things, and well as undertake formal quests and engage in duels or battles.

1.1 TYPES OF ONLINE MULTIPLAYER GAMES

Refining categories proposed by Roger Caillois, Gonzalo Frasca (2003), suggest that electronic games can be described as either *ludus* or *paidia*. Ludic virtual worlds are ruled-based games involving direct competition between players, whereas paidic worlds emphasize free play and creativity with less emphasis on rule-constrained competition.

At the ludic end of the spectrum stands *EVE Online*, in which the chief activity of advanced players is warfare where one corporation of players seeks to seize or defend solar systems of a vast galaxy against other corporations of players. At the paidic end of the spectrum stands *Tale in the Desert*, a virtual ancient Egypt in which people mainly do work of the kind real people might have done in the land of the Nile thousands of years ago, and direct aggression by one player against another is outlawed. Most popular multiplayer games fall between these extremes, and they give players considerable freedom whether they personally want to emphasize the ludic or paidic qualities of the virtual environment. However, a great variety of multiplayer online games exists or are emerging, with some but not all the characteristics of MMORPGs, in such rough categories as the following.

Strategy games differ from MMORPGs chiefly in limiting the number of players interacting with each other, currently from two to sixteen, depending on the game, and by representing the user by something like an army or an economic system, rather than by a single avatar. The historical model for strategy games is the highest-prestige board game, chess; although, the online strategy games that emphasize economic exchange can count Monopoly as their ancestor. A good example is *Warcraft: Orcs versus Humans*, the ancestor of *World of Warcraft* but limited to two players who control a number of soldiers who not only battle each other directly but also seize territory and resources to build up their relative strength. The analogy in chess is that a skilled player seeks to achieve a good position for his or her pieces, quite apart from capturing the opponent's pieces. The space-oriented younger sister of *Warcraft*, *StarCraft*, innovated by having three competing forces, and *Warcraft III* had four. Computerized strategy games often let the user play solo, competing with simple artificial intelligence built into the game, thereby building up skills, before going online to play against other people.

Non-game virtual worlds are in some respects the opposite of strategy games because they use the online environment primarily for cooperative rather than competitive purposes. *Second Life* is a well-known example (Rymaszewski et al., 2007), but others include *There*, *Active Worlds*, and *Entropia Universe*. Most of the content of *Second Life* is user-created, and the chief source of revenue for the company that hosts it is payment for virtual land on which companies, educational institutions, government agencies, and dedicated individuals build their own virtual architecture. A script-based programming language and built-in three-dimensional graphic tools allow people to build their own objects that actually perform complex functions, and some individuals try to make a living selling virtual goods. Group meetings are often held, including formal classes, business and scientific conferences, and even birthday parties, at which each user is represented by an avatar.

In contrast to *Second Life*, *Entropia Universe* gives users little power to manufacture things, but they can own property and conduct business while there are also gamelike elements such as hunting virtual animals and escaped robots. Both *Second Life* and *Entropia Universe* have special in-world currencies but allow conversion to and from dollars or other conventional forms of money. Over the years, *Entropia Universe* has experimented with various schemes in which people would treat the environment as their real world, for example, selling a space station resort for $100,000 to an enthusiast for this virtual world who called it Club Neverdie and thinking he could make a profit renting space in it. That hope was apparently not fulfilled, and when *Entropia Universe* went through a huge transformation in August 2009, switching to a more advanced graphics engine and completely recreating all the virtual environments, Club Neverdie became inaccessible. Similarly, most parts of the New Oxford cultural center of this virtual planet vanished, including the art museum depicted in Figure 1.1 at the time when it was displaying works uploaded by residents. *Entropia Universe* is an interesting and valiant attempt to explore a range of possibilities for virtual worlds, and it illustrates the challenging possibilities for evolution along the ludic-paidic spectrum, and between play and reality altogether.

Microgames is a placeholder term for a range of small multiplayer online games that may come to have a variety of names as they diversify and consolidate in the coming years. Some have qualities of the other types, but they are distinguished simply by the fact that they are modest in their demands for time and in the environment they offer. For example, *Travian* is a browser-based Medieval society strategy game with very simple two-dimensional graphics, which the user can have running simultaneously with other software, hopping over to it every few minutes or hours to make a couple of moves. Many small games run on cellphones, and others run off social networking sites such as FaceBook and MySpace. It is technically possible to integrate microgames with an MMORPG in the near future. For example, a fantasy gamefan could complete some minor activity via cellphone while riding home on the bus, such as mining virtual metal and using blacksmithing skills to make a sword out of it, then wield that sword in combat later on a high-quality desktop machine.

Figure 1.1: The New Oxford Art Museum in *Entropia Universe*.

Live action role-playing games (LARPs). These are like MMORPGs, except conducted in the "real world" rather than over Internet, but many experiments have been carried out in recent years that augmented real-world with online elements (Walther, B., 2005; Jonsson et al., 2006). One often hears that this genre emerged in the 1970s, influenced by *Dungeons and Dragons*, but arguably, it can be traced back much farther, to Capture the Flag and even to the first military training mock battles that must have originated in ancient times. With ubiquitous Internet connectivity, and mobile access through cellphones or PDAs, it is possible this genre could grow into a major industry, possibly integrated with traditional activities such as history-oriented tourism, nature trail hiking, or stock market trading. The main point to keep in mind here is that the possibility of accessing Internet anywhere at any time opens vast territory which future game innovators will explore, integrating online games with other more mundane activities.

1.2   PRESERVING GAME HISTORY

It is crucial to note that online gaming has a past as well as a future, and the current popularity of a game does not precisely measure its value for students and researchers. Consider the analogy with literature. Professors rightly do not assign their students to read the top ten novels on the current best-seller list, but select works that were published across many decades and even centuries because qualities of style, content, or historical significance outweigh their contemporary lack of popularity. Ideally, this would be true for multiplayer online games as well, but there exists no library of out-of-print worlds, nor academic publishing houses that reissue old games. Yet already, some of the very most interesting examples have ceased to exist, notably *Uru*, *Matrix Online*, and *Tabula Rasa*.

Uru was the multi-player online version of the highly innovative solo-player computer game, *Myst*, and one version of it was called *Myst Online*. The original game in the series, *Myst*, was released in 1993, and *Uru* was the fourth game in the series, coming at a time when technological possibilities had expanded considerably and multiplayer online games seemed to be the logical next step. A multiplayer beta-test version of *Uru* was opened in late 2003, and about 10,000 people entered it, only to become refugees when this beta was closed down early in 2004, and the game was sold as a solo-player game like the earlier ones in the series. A series of developments gave the passionate *Uru* refugees temporary opportunities to experience online play as the publishers experimented with multiplayer versions of the game. Furthermore, Pearce, C. (2010) studied this complex case for five years, calling it "The Uru Diaspora." Using ethnographic research methods, she observed refugees attempt to recreate the *Uru* world in two non-game virtual worlds, *There.com* and *Second Life*. In her writings about this case, Pearce argues convincingly that researchers should not become confined within a single popular game, but study relationships across multiple games and recognize that some of the unpopular ones may be especially worthy targets for research.

Matrix Online (MxO) was a more-or-less successful online game that lasted from March 2005 through July 2009 (McCubbin, C., 2005; Bainbridge, W., 2010a). Based on the popular trilogy of movies, which started with the widely acclaimed *The Matrix* in 1999, MxO was set two centuries in the future within a computer simulation of a 1999 city. Partly inspired by the book *Simulacra and Simulation* by social philosopher Baudrillard, J. (1994), the *Matrix* series engaged issues of false consciousness, the illusory nature of social conventions, exploitation of workers by capitalists, and existential doubts about the reality of the physical world. Unfortunately, the logical result of this train of thought made the city a rather disturbing and confining place, from which the player could never escape. Yet, the city in *Matrix Online* was a very impressive accomplishment, visually and intellectually – vast, realistic, and filled with interesting architectural ideas – in fifty-two substantial neighborhoods from the filthy slums to the awe-inspiring business district. Hosted by Sony, but not created using Sony's technology and thus incompatible with its other online multiplayer games, MxO may have been a burden to maintain. At the time MxO closed, Sony offered a subscription plan in which a player got access to an entire suite of games for the price of subscribing to any two, and after a sufficient number of other games were available, Sony may have felt that maintaining MxO was of no commercial advantage.

Figure 1.2 shows a scene from *Tabula Rasa* that illustrates its fundamental premise and complexity. Created by a team led by Richard Garriott, a leader in the history of these games and the son of an astronaut, TR begins with the premise that an ancient extraterrestrial species has split into two factions, the possibly benevolent Eloh and the power-hungry Neph. Using advanced technology, the Neph have launched an army against many solar systems, already defeating the Earth and now fighting the remnants of our forces on two other planets, Foreas and Arieki, where humans have gained alliances with the local intelligent species. This picture illustrates the conflict because a battle is taking place in the background, fought with ray guns against force shields, and the two aircraft are delivering Neph soldiers to the fray. But it also illustrates two more intellectual themes, the search for knowledge and the development of technology. The two levitating pylons are Eloh artifacts, inscribed with glowing hieroglyphics in the Eloh language called *Logos*, which the player must acquire through exploration and which confer advanced powers. The figure at the right is the main character's clone, a secondary avatar that can be created only once when certain Logos elements and other resources have been acquired.

Many games have aspects of conflict, questing, and crafting valuable new items or even creating secondary avatars. What makes *Tabula Rasa* almost unique was that it couched them in terms of an idealistic, real-world mission to seek wisdom by exploring the universe. In October 2008, just before the closure of *Tabula Rasa* was announced against his wishes, Richard Garriott actually rocketed to the orbiting International Space Station, delivering a memory unit containing all the TR avatars, mine included. Given how interesting and even fun I found *Tabula Rasa* to be, it is hard for me to avoid the conclusions that many current gameplayers lack the intellectual sophistication to appreciate the cultural depth some of the best games achieve and that popularity does not correlate with philosophical significance.

1.3   INTELLECTUAL APPROACHES TO GAMES

Potentially, each of the social sciences and many fields of the humanities could be applied to online gaming, but here we will seek an integrated approach that also relies upon computer and information science. While some traditional social science has been written, most of the extant scholarly literature is in one or both of two traditions: (1) game studies and (2) human-centered computing. Specialists in this area also need to draw upon two kinds of mostly non-scholarly literature: (1) game instruction manuals whether produced by professionals or amateurs (e.g., Lummis and Kern (2006)), and (2) trade books in some way connected to game design (e.g., Prensky, M. (2001)).

As the website of the National Science Foundation explains, "Human Centered Computing (HCC) research explores creative ideas, novel theories, and innovative technologies that advance our understanding of the complex and increasingly coupled relationships between people and computing"[1]. A report of an NSF-funded workshop about HCC observes (Sears et al., 2008, p. 8):

---

[1] http://www.nsf.gov/funding/pgm_summ.jsp?pims_id=503302&org=IIS

Figure 1.2: A *Tabula Rasa* exobiologist and his clone.

Multiplayer online gaming produces new cultures, social norms, and communication mechanisms. Understanding how these social aspects of games develop, as well as what causes individuals to become engaged in these virtual communities, could prove useful in other social computing contexts. For example, it would be useful to understand how certain social norms are established, what kind of interaction the members of the community are engaged in, and how specific communication mechanisms can be encouraged as new online communication mechanisms and online communities are developed to support work-related activities, distance education, and various other applications.

Klastrup, L. (2009) has argued that multiplayer online games must be considered as multi-dimensional worlds, for which no single analytical approach will suffice:

For instance, we can successfully analyse an "old world" like *EverQuest* as a game and learn a lot about the functions of this world by looking, for instance, at the game mechanics and the type of goals and challenges the players are presented with. But in doing so we might not understand why players choose to engage themselves exactly in *EverQuest* and not any other gameworld. One might also look at a gameworld like *EverQuest* primarily as a social culture by looking, for instance, at how people in *EverQuest* socially interact with each other and for which reasons, but then we might not be able to explain why some players enjoy playing a world mostly by themselves.

In her own analysis, Klastrup identifies three distinct ways of understanding gameworlds that would need to be combined to give a full picture:

1. Fictions: a form of make-believe in which users willingly suspend their disbelief in the reality of the gameworld.

2. Narratives: meaningful presentations of a series of events within a symbolic frame of reference.

3. Interpretations: representations of "what a world is or should look like."

I suggest that traditional *fictions* differed from today's gameworlds in two ways that could be described as grammatic: they were told in the past tense and the third person. Once upon a time, Robin Hood dwelled in the Sherwood forest with his merry men, yet at this very moment, Orastes is preparing to have his picture taken sitting on his horse in front of the temple of Mitra in the Aquilonian hamlet called Tesso. Orastes is a character from the Conan stories written in the 1930s by Robert E. Howard, which tell of a land long lost in the mists of time, yet he lives today as one of my characters in *Age of Conan*. One might argue that much science fiction is set in future tense, yet the stories are almost always written in the past tense – future perfect tense if you insist – as if they had already happened. At experience level 50, Orastes has completed the research tasks I have set for him, but until I cancel my game subscription, he can live again in present tense, allowing me to experience his adventures in realtime, moment to moment.

A few traditional fiction stories are written in first person, like autobiographies, but, typically, they are written in the third person, about "him" or "her." Consider this sentence: "Hither came Conan, the Cimmerian, black-haired, sullen-eyed, sword in hand, a thief, a reaver, a slayer, with gigantic melancholies and gigantic mirth, to tread the jeweled thrones of the Earth under his sandaled feet"[2]. This is the last sentence of the first paragraph of Howard's first Conan story, "The Phoenix on the Sword," but it pretends to be a quotation from an ancient book called *The Nemedian Chronicles*. It introduces Conan to the reader, a powerful barbarian with only the most primitive sense of honor, quite different from the reader however much the reader may come to identify with him. In contrast, when I was a small child, my father used to invent stories about a fox who lived in the woods near our house, named Peters Foxy. But instead of telling them in a simple third person, about how Peters Foxy saved the other foxes when the floods came, my father narrated in the second person, describing what I did to help my fox friend. In this case, my father told me I had instructed the foxes to take the mattresses from their beds and float around on them as if they were rafts. Online games

[2] http://gutenberg.net.au/ebooks06/0600811.txt

are, to a significant degree, fictions in the second person because they are about *your* experiences and accomplishments; although, this is one of the area's most intense, scholarly debates, how much the players really identify with their characters and take the initiative that would render the games first-person narratives.

Traditional *narratives* tell stories in a linear fashion through time, from a set of starting conditions to a satisfying conclusion (Abbott, H., 2003, 2008). Typically, a hero seeks to achieve a goal, against opposition but usually with allies, through a series of episodes or chapters (each of which is a brief narrative). The human mind likes goal-directed narrative structures, presumably because this style of thought evolved to serve our daily needs for food and shelter, and then transferred over into literature. This linear structure often applies to single-player videogames and computer games, for instance, in *Chronicles of Riddick* in which the protagonist's sole goal is to escape from prison. The nice irony of that example is that whenever Riddick does temporarily escape, he is always recaptured, and most of the time he has no choices whatsoever concerning what he must do next. Many fiction authors have experimented with alternatives to the traditional linear narrative, yet it prevails. Samuel R. Delany's novel *Dhalgren* is circular, concluding with the beginning of the sentence that ends on the first page. The protagonist in Samuel Beckett's *Malone Dies* attempts to cast away all his memories, so he can cease to exist before death claims him, yet his emotions become aroused and he dies unwilling to let go of his past. Numerous novels employ flashbacks, and some experiment with moving backward in time, yet is hard to name any successful work of traditional fiction literature that does not rely heavily upon linear narrative from a start to a finish, perhaps partly, because books are bound from first page to last.

Much has been made of the non-linear character of role-playing games (Rouse, R., 2001), but this does not mean they avoid narrative, merely that the player has a considerable range of choices across multiple parallel narratives. Every gamelike virtual world has a *backstory*, a narrative that describes how the fictional world came to be. In the case of *World of Warcraft*, it is provided by the three previous *Warcraft* strategy games, and in the case of *Star Wars Galaxies*, it is provided by the four movies that are set in time prior to when the game events take place in the larger *Star Wars* narrative. The games tend to emphasize quests or missions, each of which is a brief narrative the player must act out correctly in order to get credit, although there is great choice which quest to do next and exactly how to complete it. The larger narrative structure in most such games is actually highly linear, the progress up the ladder of experience levels which is required to gain access to many features of the virtual world. Even *Entropia Universe*, which lacks missions and has no single measure of experience, requires players to advance along several pre-defined experience tracks in order to exploit the virtual world successfully, such as strength of armor, weapons, and hunting skill needed to defend against the ubiquitous nasty animals.

Klastrup defines the *interpretation* dimension of gamelike virtual worlds somewhat broadly, suggesting that, at the very least, each of them needs to harmonize with what human beings expect a world to be. However, many of the games, arguably even all of them, also serve as interpretations of the particular "real world" we actually inhabit.

1.4 RESEARCH TOPIC AREAS

In their 2007 survey of massively multiplayer online games, Achterbosch et al. (2007) reported that the literature in this field chiefly covered four topic areas:

(1) The social interactions between players.

(2) The different architectures to build MMORPGs.

(3) The effects of latency. (Internet delay time.)

(4) Problems that plague MMORPGs.

Except for the third of these, latency, these categories could be defined very broadly to cover a variety of things, but the authors seem to construe them fairly narrowly. For example, under *problems*, they list specifically these security issues: "... cheating within the game to gain an unfair advantage; hacking an account and using it illegally; and counterfeiting documents to obtain an account illegally." Some of my own research falls into the first category, social interactions between players, but I also do research in two areas not covered by any of these four where I believe there is already considerable literature:

(5) Relations between a player and his or her avatars or characters.

(6) The cultural content of the game.

In the pages that follow, we will see much research that does not fit comfortably even in these six categories, and it would require us to construct a longer list or start the categorization process over again with broader concepts. For example, many researchers have been looking at the different personalities and motivations of players. Others are studying the economics both internal to the games, and external where games compete in the marketplace, and these researchers might not want to classify their topic as "social interactions." In addition, there is much literature concerning the computer graphics required to display the gameworlds and characters on the computer screen, and some of this connects to human beings, either because it relies upon how the human brain reacts to different visualization techniques or because the graphics need to depict the human body as it engages in various actions and gestures.

In computer science, the term *architecture* tends to be applied to large-scale design decisions, but there are also many smaller-scale design decisions that are worthy of study. I am particularly interested in the techniques for operating secondary avatars, such as the hunting animals used by hunter characters in *World of Warcraft*, and many other researchers have focused on the (admittedly simple) artificial intelligence techniques developed to operate non-player characters (Maher et al., 2005; Merrick and Maher, 2006; Moriarty and Gonzalez, 2009).

Similarly, problems come in all sizes, and many of them relate to social interactions and architecture, as well as to details of game design. One of the more challenging sets of examples concerns the auction systems in which players buy and sell virtual items, including products of gathering and crafting professions. Every game I have tried that has one of these uses a somewhat different user interface, distinctive search tools, unique pricing and bidding rules, and, in some cases, restrictions on which characters are allowed to use which part of the system. A problem that might be described as social afflicts games that are not very popular, namely a lack of items for sale that might be worth buying, simply because there are too few players posting things for sale. I found this in both *Matrix Online* and *Tabula Rasa*, both of which were shut down soon after I finished my research on them. *Matrix Online* tried to compensate by placing some items in the auction system automatically, and the very good auction system in *EVE Online* seemed to have little to do with what individual players were selling. Automatic operation of an economic system requires very careful design, and it, indeed, may require constant adjustment to prevent the system from spiraling out of control.

CHAPTER 2

Historical-Cultural Origins

Today's games cannot be fully understood without a knowledge of the history of online gaming. Castronova, E. (2003) offered an early sketch of this history, for example, noting the importance of *Dungeons and Dragons* as a pre-Internet influence and citing the early examples of *Ultima Online* in 1997 and *Lineage* in 1998, but much research will need to be done before we can confidently chart the most important influences. For example, the notion that the fantasy stories of J. R. R. Tolkien were very influential reflects widespread awareness of Tolkien's work among the general public, while Tolkien was probably a very minor influence within this specialized field because creators of the games were deeply familiar with a much older and deeper tradition of heroic fantasy stories by many authors.

Thus, it is also important to understand what might be called the *pre-history of online games*: the deeply rooted subcultures and artistic genres on which the entire field is based. A big part of the cultural content of any particular game is what players call *lore*, the mythology and legends of the game, which often are created by the game designers afresh, although influenced indirectly by the earlier work of other people. A coherent and compelling mythic story is required to make the world come alive and draw the player into it. In a study of how this has been done successfully in *World of Warcraft*, Krzywinska, T. (2006, p. 383) argues that "the mythic plays a primary role in making a consistent fantasy world in terms of game play, morality, culture, times, and environment. It provides a rationale for players' actions, as well as the logic that underpins the stylistic profile of the game, its objects, tasks, and characters."

A Tale in the Desert is a good example of a gamelike virtual world based on actual human history because it seeks to replicate ancient Egypt, with an emphasis on the technology and socio-cultural structure. *Dark Age of Camelot* draws, to some extent, upon real European history, but it draws even more intensely upon the folklore of Dark Ages societies. Some games recycle or build upon stories, characters, and concepts developed for another medium, notably novels and movies. Examples include *Age of Conan*, based upon Robert E. Howard's Conan stories, *Star Wars Galaxies* based on the movies by George Lucas, and *Lord of the Rings Online* based on J. R. R. Tolkien's novels and on the movies based on the novels. This dimension of culture can be studied from an anthropological perspective or from the perspective of literature and dramatic arts. But it also has profound implications for how we understand the game and what it offers to players.

2.1   *A TALE IN THE DESERT*

The little-known treasure among online games is *Tale in the Desert*, a charming and educationally valuable depiction of ancient Egypt that has far fewer players than it deserves. This is not to say that it depicts ancient life with perfect accuracy, but it does capture the spirit of the past in a way that communicates some real facts. The world represents a large but, admittedly, somewhat reduced model of the Nile valley where the focus is on building a virtual society and gaining knowledge of the environment, rather than fighting. Indeed, although players may compete to accomplish various feats, there is absolutely no violent combat. Much of the action involves solving puzzles, building things that are beyond the capacity of any one individual, and conducting rituals that require two or more people.

My research was done during the fourth *telling* of this tale, which is restarted with new features every year or two. I built a home on the east bank of the Nile in the center of the country, joined three guilds because multiple guild membership is permitted, began raising sheep, and started constructing tools for manufacturing. Frankly, a good deal of the technology looks like the nineteenth century AD, rather than BC, but it offers an excellent metaphor of technology in general, including the necessity of establishing a complex system of resource supply and product manufacturing. Many players may find this game boring because, for example, building a house to complete one of the earliest missions requires to first make a thousand bricks, but that may realistically reflect the fact that it was hard work to survive in the ancient world.

The game's own newbie-zone introduction provides the best example for present purposes. My character, Ren Hotep, began on an isolated island, with the task of gaining the skills and materials needed to build a boat to sail to the Egyptian mainland. He started with practically nothing. Walking along the shore, he occasionally found a piece of slate rock, and banging two of them together often fractured one in just the right way to create a cutting blade. One stone blade and four additional pieces of slate can make a wood plane to turn wood gathered from the nearby trees into boards, although the blade breaks occasionally and needs to be replaced.

It sounds simple to make a boat because the materials needed are 20 pieces of wood, 20 boards, 4 ropes, 4 units of tar, and a sail. The tar can be collected easily from a small tar pit, although the player needs to hunt all over the island to find it. The sail is graciously provided, so that leaves only the rope. This is where the plot thickens because making rope turns out to require a huge number of gathering and crafting steps. The rope must be made from flax, and the player receives a gift consisting of flax seeds. So far, so good. Planting the seeds, weeding the garden, and waiting until the flax can be harvested takes a little patience, but the real problem is that one unit of seeds produces one unit of flax, consuming all the seeds. To get enough seeds, the player needed to plant some but avoid weeding, and then wait until the flax has gone to seed, which yields a profit in seeds. With practice, Ren Hotep could manage four little gardens at once, but had to do some over and over again, building up his stock of seeds, then investing them in growing flax.

The next step is to release the fibers from the flax plant. The technical term for the method used is *retting*, but the game calls it *rotting*, which is also factually correct and more familiar. The flax is placed in water, where microorganisms go to work on it. Ren Hotep would drop a bundle of newly harvested flax into a nearby stream, and he would wait. The next step, separating the retted flax into its components, requires a flax comb. Unfortunately, the flax combs in the game are substantial devices, requiring 18 boards, 60 thorns, and 36 bricks to build. Ren made more boards with his plane, and he gathered thorns for nearby bushes, but what about the bricks?

Bricks can be made from mud, sand, and straw. Mud and sand can be gathered from different kinds of soil, but straw must be made from grass. The process was simple: gather grass, drop it in bundles on the ground, and they will dry into straw under the blazing Egyptian sun. The need for straw was clearly stated in the Bible, Exodus 5:7, where Pharaoh punishes the Israelites by saying, "Ye shall no more give the people straw to make brick, as heretofore: let them go and gather straw for themselves." These components must be assembled in a brick rack, made from four boards and liable to break after several uses. One of the components of flax, tow, can be spun into twine, and twine can be spun into rope. This requires a small distaff, which is made from 10 pieces of wood, 12 boards, and fully 100 bricks. Figure 2.1 shows the three major pieces of equipment: the wood plane (center foreground), flax comb (left), and small distaff (background).

All three of these machines are far larger and more complex than the average ancient Egyptian would have used. Well-cut boards were probably rare in ancient times, and they were formed by saws rather than planes. A flax comb, often technically called a heckling comb, was also worked by hand, whereas the one in the game operates by itself. Even in recent centuries a distaff was a small stick used for manual fiber working, and here it seems to have been combined with a rather formidable spinning wheel. Probably, it would have been difficult for the game designers to work out the detailed graphics needed to show skilled hand work with comb and distaff, and the machines they came up with were marvelous to watch in operation as historically incorrect as they may be.

The fundamental lessons of this introduction to ancient Egypt are actually rather profound. Starting with nothing at the dawn of history, the human species needed to bootstrap its technology to a complex level, in order to support a populous and complex society. To do so, humans needed to invent tools, including tools to make tools, investing in the physical capital needed for economic production. Many processes needed to be carried out in a precise series of steps, following plans that modern computer scientists would call algorithms. First, plant the seeds, then harvest the flax, then rot it, then run it through a comb, then spin the resultant tow into twine, then spine the twine into rope. Everything that happens in a computer game depends on how humans interact with algorithms, but perhaps that is also true for "real life."

2.2 DARK AGE OF CAMELOT

Some games take history very seriously without attempting to duplicate past eras accurately. A good example is *Dark Age of Camelot*, which is set in a period shortly after the death of King Arthur during the western European Dark Ages (Mylonas, E., 2005). The world is divided into three separate cultures which are at war with each other. Albion is the English society of Arthur's legacy, and Camelot is its capital city. Midgard is the Viking society, representing Scandinavian and Teutonic traditions, and it has a capital named Jordheim that does not seem to correspond to any historical place. Hibernia represents Celtic folklore, named after but not limited to Ireland, and its capital is Tir na Nog, a mythical place in Celtic legends about an Otherworld that exists over the

Figure 2.1: Ren Hotep Making Rope in *Tale in the Desert*.

sea, under the ground, or on a supernatural plane of existence. Figure 2.2 shows a Viking visiting Stonehenge in Albion, a member of one of these warring societies acting as a peaceful tourist in one of the others. This was possible for her only because she exists on the one "cooperative" server in which the three realms are at peace with each other.

The game's Wikipedia article suggests that Albion is the most historically accurate. Hibernia is the least accurate, and Midgard falls between them:

Albion is based on Arthurian legend, with such notable real-world places as Hadrian's Wall, Stonehenge, and other locations in Great Britain. The races and classes of Albion, in the original game and early expansions, tended to be more professions and peoples of European history and mythology than inventions of the gamemakers. Hibernia is based

Figure 2.2: A Viking Visiting Stonehenge in *Dark Age of Camelot*.

on Celtic folklore and the landscape includes lush green rolling hills typical of Ireland. Although the quest storylines, place names, and numerous game elements are firmly fixed in Celtic mythology, Hibernian races and classes are typically the creation of the gamemakers. Midgard is based on Norse mythology and its landscape includes misty fjords and pine forests... The adherence of the architecture to the forms and design of medieval and pre-medieval Norse architecture is notable[1].

Both Camelot and Stonehenge are the centers of elaborate legends, mythologies, and occult speculations, yet clearly Stonehenge is real, and Camelot may have been as well. As it happens, I visited Stonehenge twice, and the first time (in 1965), it was still permissible to touch the stones to verify their reality. It is possible I may have visited Camelot as well, although I cannot test this hypothesis empirically. Archaeologists, historians, and folklore enthusiasts have speculated that a

[1]http://en.wikipedia.org/wiki/Dark_Age_of_Camelot; retrieved September 19, 2009.

small number of sites in England might have been Camelot, and one of them is Cadbury Castle in Somerset. In 1984, I tramped around this completely ruined hill fort, recognizable only by its surviving perimeter wall, wondering where I was in history. The story of King Arthur is especially interesting because there really may have been such a person, although living in an illiterate society that did not record the facts of his life, and his current Wikipedia page nicely summarizes the debates about him[2]. If Arthur lived in the Dark Ages, written stories of his exploits do not date until much later, in the Middle Ages or even early Renaissance. The lack of contemporary written records does not prove he and his city were fables, but it leaves us wondering. Camelot is a lot like Troy, a city that was remembered in Homeric Greek legends but not confirmed until Heinrich Schliemann excavated the site in the 1870s, except we may never have proof in the case of Camelot.

The standard image of Camelot today is the one that writers hundreds of years ago believed in, and *Dark Age of Camelot* depicts it as a late Medieval castle town, more than a Dark Ages citadel. This kind of anachronism is quite common in popular histories, seeing the distant past from the point of view of the more recent past. This phenomenon deserves a technical name. I rather like the term *vector*, because in computer science, it can refer to a dynamic data array, and in mathematics, it often refers to representations that have both length and direction. Given all the many meanings already attached to *vector*, introducing one more usage cannot increase the confusion. A *vector history* is one that looks at a particular point in past time from another, later point in past time, or from a different culture. Note that in doing a vector history, we select a point of view (in time and cultural space) that is not our own, and we then look at a third point in human history from that perspective.

This kind of relativity is illustrated in several ways by Figure 2.2 The version of Stonehenge depicted in the game is not very different from the real one, perhaps a little wider but having many of the same features. At the time of King Arthur – assuming he lived in the real Dark Ages – Stonehenge was already perhaps three thousand years old. Some of the legends say it was built by Merlin using magic. Supernatural power was not required to raise the stones, but it certainly would have been required to do so in the distant past, long before the magician was born! Modern adherents of Druidic religions like to think it was a temple of their ancient ancestors, and many quests in the game require fighting Druids, but realistically even the Druidism encountered by the ancient Romans may have arisen when Stonehenge was two thousand years old. *Dark Age of Camelot* depicts Stonehenge in nearly mint condition, and none of its stones have yet fallen down. The lone stone on the horizon in the picture, possibly the famous "heel stone" and defended by Druid magicians, currently leans at an angle, as I confirmed in 1965 by leaning on it, but the game shows it still standing fully upright. The Zone of the game where Stonehenge is found carries the correct name, Salisbury Plain, and it possesses a number of other ancient circular trenches and standing stones, although I have not yet located the virtual equivalents of two other spectacular nearby sites, Avebury and Silbury Hill. Well, one of the circles of standing stones look very much like Avebury, but without a label, how can I tell if it really "is?"

---

[2]http://en.wikipedia.org/wiki/King_Arthur; retrieved September 19, 2009.

The Viking in the picture is my valkyrie, Reitsche, and her vector perspective is cross-cultural more than anachronistic. To their credit, the creators of *Dark Age of Camelot* have used a large number of Scandinavian names and words for the Midgard faction, as well as folklore elements, but the dominant modern image of valkyries is German, notably the familiar music to the Ride of the Valkyries in Richard Wagner's opera, *Die Walküre.* The opera actually contains nine valkyries, so when I was creating this character, I methodically entered the name of each one, discovering somebody else had already taken it for their valkyrie character. With Wagner's music running through my mind, I tried to think of yet another valkyrie name, and the best I could do was remember the actual heroic German woman test pilot, Hannah Reitsch, adding a final "e" to make it like the other valkyrie names. This seemed a logical choice, given that she was the first woman to pilot a helicopter, a jet fighter plane, and an honest-to-goodness rocket ship. Notice again the vector history. Many players selected names from a nineteenth-century German opera, and I selected the name of a twentieth-century German, to name a Scandinavian character from perhaps the eighth century.

2.3   *AGE OF CONAN*

The Conan stories are based on the clever conceit that many aspects of ancient European and Egyptian culture were remnants of an even earlier age that has been entirely forgotten, that itself was built upon the ruins of the even earlier period in which Atlantis flourished. Like *Dark Age of Camelot*, *Age of Conan* depicts three separate cultures, although one difference is that they are not at war with each other. Stygia represents ancient Egypt, Aquilonia represents the Roman Empire, and Cimmeria represents Celtic traditions but also barbarism more generally. This scheme allowed Robert E. Howard to draw upon ancient history without being a slave to it and to imbue his stories with intense emotionality despite their scholarly framework.

In recent years, both social science and computer science have rediscovered emotion. In his presidential address to the American Sociological Association, Massey, D. (2002) explained that emotion is an integral part of social interaction and of individual cognition, and thus it cannot be ignored in any serious analysis of human behavior. The term *affective computing* is widely applied to methods that endow computers with the ability to recognize and to respond realistically to human emotions (Picard, R., 1997; Peter and Beale, 2008).

The emotions expressed in the Conan stories are chiefly rage, lust, and terror, although Conan himself is incapable of feeling fear. In the technical meaning of the term, these are *immoral* stories, because Conan is allowed to kill other people merely to serve his own self-interest or express his momentary impulses. It is worth contemplating the extent to which this immoral ethic exists in many MMORPGs because the player is often required to kill non-player characters or even characters operated by other players, merely to advance in the game. Morality aside, the Conan stories are *psychiatric* and can suggest principles from depth psychology because they sprang from the arguably pathological personality of the author.

At the age of thirty, in 1936, when told his mother was about to die, Robert E. Howard killed himself. Although he exercised physically to gain at least a fraction of Conan's brute strength, emotionally he was a child tied to the apron strings of his mother, and he had promised her as early as age six that the two of them would always live and die together (De Camp et al., 1983). Although he wrote stories about ancient history and exotic nations, he had little higher education and hardly ever left his native Texas. Thus, the Conan stories are the extreme in vicarious compensation for real-world deficiencies, the ultimate in escapism. A popular slogan in the science-fiction subculture says, "Science fiction is escape... into reality." We may well ask to what extent today's multiplayer online games are also escapist, versus legitimate exploration of an emerging new reality.

There is an even deeper level of analysis suggested by the case of Conan, a kind of historical psychoanalysis. It is remarkable how many of Sigmund Freud's writings are historical in focus, and, arguably, psychoanalysis is about two intertwined pasts: the cultural history of humanity and the psychological history of the individual. Indeed, psychoanalysis itself may already be an historical artifact because its theories are based heavily upon the family experience of a certain class of people in Austria a century ago, in which fathers were powerful, whereas in Howard's case, the mother was powerful. The key psychoanalytic publication that brings together history and personality is Freud's 1930 book *Civilization and its Discontents*, arguing that the wide sweep of history has required individuals to subordinate their personal impulses more and more to society's demands, leading to frustration, inhibition, and widespread neurosis. Conan smashes civilization with his sledgehammer, achieving the triumph of desire over discretion. Ironically, the violence in multiplayer online games may represent the liberation of rage that has been suppressed by civilization, using the most civilized of technologies to unleash primitive forces.

2.4   *LORD OF THE RINGS ONLINE*

Everybody knows that *Lord of the Rings Online* is based on a novel by J. R. R. Tolkien, *The Hobbit*, and on his *Lord of the Rings* trilogy, but people may not be widely aware of what that means for the values embedded in the game. On the one hand, Tolkien was a professor of historical linguistics, philology, and literature, so his creative works of fantasy are based on far more scholarly erudition than is usually the case. On the other hand, his works are in a deep sense religious allegories. A Roman Catholic, he was also conversant with the Protestant and Anglican traditions, and approached Christianity in the manner that highly educated but devout members of English culture often do, with a poetic detachment and sense of aesthetic grandeur.

Conventional religion is underrepresented in videogames and online virtual worlds (Bainbridge and Bainbridge, 2007a). Given the fact that two of the three popular videogame system companies are Japanese (Playstation and Nintendo), diluted versions of Asian religions are found in many games. Occasionally, sectarian or speculative versions of conventional western religions creep in, for example, in the videogame version of *The Da Vinci Code*. However, most religious references in multiplayer online games concern pagan religions of the past, religious cults, or fantasy religions similar in many respects to ancient polytheistic religions. A striking exception is the videogame version of *The Chronicles of Narnia: the Lion, the Witch, and the Wardrobe*, based on a novel by Tolkien's close friend C. S. Lewis, which explicitly teaches love and respect by making the player operate four characters who are children of the same family and who must cooperate to succeed.

The trilogy of novels, *Lord of the Rings*, concerns a battle between good and evil, focused on assembling and using a ring of immense magical power. Even the best and most moral heroes become seduced by the possibility of gaining personal power with the ring, but in the end it is destroyed and balance is restored to the Earth. Players in *Lord of the Rings Online* gain many of the abilities of players in other games, such as *World of Warcraft*, but they are not couched in magical terms. For example, Rumilisoun, my elf lore-master, does not cast spells at enemies, but hurls hot coals at them, which has exactly the same effect but does not violate conservative Christian prohibitions against practicing magic. Over the centuries, Christianity has struggled with the issue that belief in supernatural powers implies the possibility of monopolizing some of them for one's selfish benefit, and its general response has been to reject magic and rely upon God's grace instead (Stark and Bainbridge, 1985, 1987). Figure 2.3 shows Rumilisoun visiting her friends the Hobbits in The Shire.

Figure 2.3: An Elf Visits the Hobbits in *Lord of the Rings Online*.

Elves, in Tolkien's world, are essentially immortal, although they tend to behave more like detached philosophers than like angels. Hobbits, like the one walking just behind Rumilisoun, are modest people, living modest and limited lives, but who have long dwelled peacefully in The Shire, which expresses one traditional view of "Merrie Olde England." However, The Shire may represent another mythical land, in that, it lacks any church or temple. Where in all of human history was there never a church, temple, synagogue, or mosque? Answer: the Garden of Eden. If one lives perfectly in harmony with fellow beings and with God, there is no need of religion. Thus, unlike many of the other virtual worlds described here, *Lord of the Rings Online* largely lack religious institutions, not because it is secular, but precisely because it is in its entirety a religious allegory.

The Lord of the Rings is often described as a prominent example of *high fantasy*, whereas the Conan stories are *low fantasy*. The distinction does not concern quality or cultural sophistication but the extent to which the mythos is connected to actual history and the folklore of real societies. *High fantasy*, like Tolkien's stories, is set in an entirely fictional world which is quite distinct from the real world, whereas *low fantasy* is on balance less imaginative because it includes many elements taken from the real world. Obviously, this distinction is a matter of degree. Orcs and elves were long part of European folklore, and Tolkien's hobbits seem to speak the Anglo-Saxon language and thus to be English. Another category, sometimes called *science fantasy* but more commonly called *science fiction*, gives fantasy ideas a veneer of plausibility by couching them in the metaphors of science and technology.

2.5   *STAR WARS GALAXIES*

This online multiplayer game is obviously based on the *Star Wars* movies, and it depicts familiar fictional planets such as Tatoonine and Naboo, where players have created vibrant economic and social systems that allow them to experience living in one of their favorite fantasies (Ducheneaut and Moore, 2004; Ducheneaut et al., 2007). Specifically, *Star Wars Galaxies* is set just after the action of the original 1977 movie, but three prequel movies were later made, so it falls between the fourth and fifth of the six main movies in terms of the story. Indeed, on its fifth anniversary, it gave players the opportunity to travel to a remote location and congratulate Luke Skywalker for having just destroyed the Death Star and even to inspect his rocket- propelled fighter craft. Some locales from the chronologically last movie are included, such as Jabba's fortress and the Ewok villages, but presumably these existed for years prior to their appearance in the film.

Multiplayer games based on familiar stories face a very difficult problem, in that they cannot duplicate those stories and must find other ways to exploit their settings. The reason is that it would be highly unrealistic to run the same events over and over again, with players lined up around the block to slay Darth Vader one more time. Games that are not based on popular stories have this problem of dramatic unrealism as well, but to a lesser degree because they offer very broad plots with many villains to slay in many different sequences. Solo player games do not have this problem, and an excellent example is *Star Wars Episode II: Revenge of the Sith*. The player alternates running either Obi-Wan Kenobi or Anakin Skywalker through the plot of the movie, until they meet at the end in the battle that turns the latter into Darth Vader. No other players intrude to spoil the player's sense of immersion and dramatic coherence.

Just as the game was based on a series of movies, the movies were heavily based on a pre-existing artistic genre and even to a remarkable extent on specific earlier works. In the most obvious way imaginable, the *Star Wars* movies are inspired by the *Flash Gordon* movie series of the 1930s (Kinnard, R., 1988; Gordon, A., 1995). The very opening, when paragraphs of text scroll up and away describing the previous episode of the story, is taken from the 1940 serial *Flash Gordon Conquers the Universe*, and the famous *Star Wars* music was directly inspired by the classic *Flash Gordon* soundtracks. Audiences may have been confused in the escape scene of the 1977 *Star Wars* movie, when Luke accidentally destroys the controls for a light bridge and needs to hold Leia as they swing across a chasm on a cable like Tarzan and Jane on a jungle vine. Several scenes of the 1938 serial, *Flash Gordon's Trip to Mars* involve a light bridge, including one in which the heroes escape. The *Flash Gordon* movies were based on a comic strip, which in turn was based on the *Buck Rogers* comic strip which in turn was based on serious science stories written by Philip Francis Nowlan, and *Flash Gordon* also drew on the ten influential Mars novels by Edgar Rice Burroughs.

Although no one work of literature can claim all the credit for launching the genre from which *Star Wars* drew or, indeed, for providing the mythic basis for all online fantasy games, the novels of Edgar Rice Burroughs were tremendously influential (Porges, I., 1975; Lupoff, R., 1976). Beginning with his first published story in 1911, Burroughs created a complex imaginary world, not unlike Tatooine or *World of Warcraft*. The fourth novel in the series, *Thuvia, Maid of Mars*, introduced the idea that women could be brave science-fiction warriors equally with men, and it included a glossary of Martian terms. *The Chessmen of Mars* included instructions for playing a Martian game with some affinities to *Warcraft: Orcs and Humans*. The fundamental premise has carried over into many games, including *Star Wars Galaxies*: an advanced, decaying society has reverted to feudalism with constant warfare, mixing anachronistic technologies such as swords and spaceships, and where technology blends imperceptibly with magic. Luke Skywalker's Tatooine has moisture vaporators because the planet has lost its seas, whereas Burroughs' Mars has atmosphere factories because the air is leaking away into space. Luke uses the magical Force to aim his missile at the right point on the Death Star, whereas the hero of Burroughs' first novel uses telepathy to open the locked door of the malfunctioning atmosphere system in order to save his entire world.

Most of the games described here owe a debt to the table-top game, *Dungeons and Dragons*, and D&D acknowledges its debt to writers like Burroughs who created the century-old literary genre of heroic science-fantasy that inspires even many of the most recent online games (Gygax, G., 1979). Within the science fiction literary subculture, various technical terms are used to describe different kinds of fiction (Bainbridge, W., 1986). *Star Wars* is *space opera*, whereas some of the other games are closer to *sword-and-sorcery*.

Space operas are extravagant adventures set against a fanciful interplanetary background, in which little attention is paid to scientific realism, and much of the technology functions as if by magic but usually wrapped in the rhetoric of machinery. *Sword-and-sorcery* is a variety of fantasy, typically concerning the adventures of brave heroes trekking through barbarian lands, wielding primitive weapons against demons and wizards, but sometimes including science-fiction elements as well. The point of this example is to show that a serious attempt to understand the mythos of a modern gamelike virtual world will need to take account of the older culture to which it belongs, reaching back a century and more, long predating the invention of Internet.

CHAPTER 3

Technical Constraints

Many behind-the-scenes technical details about online games can be ignored by players, but four in particular need to be understood: *latency, sharding, graphics*, and what, for want of a standard term, I call *rolecoding* and which will be covered the next section. *Latency* is the delay caused by the need to send information between each player over Internet and the central server that combines their actions and controls the game, and it is a crucial if narrow topic, as Achterbosch et al. (2007) noted. *Sharding* is the need to separate out some areas of the virtual world for selected players, either to provide them with distinctive experiences or to manage the large number of players who may be online at the moment. *Graphics* concerns how the virtual world and its contents are displayed, and here we will focus on those aspects that are especially relevant to the user's experience.

3.1 LATENCY

Griwodz and Halvorsen (2006) studied latency issues in *Anarchy Online*, which uses the standard Internet protocols, Transmission Control Protocol (TCP) and Internet Protocol (IP). This is a decades-old set of standards for transmitting packets of data, and one of its features is that it checks to see if each packet reached its destination and will resend the packet if not. This is crucial for sending documents over Internet, but it may not be entirely necessary for all information transmitted in games. A subset protocol, User Datagram Protocol (UDP), does not verify that a packet reached its destination and, therefore, tends to function more quickly if less reliably. A study of the Chinese game *ShenZhou Online*, by Chen et al. (2006), indicated that TCP was not good for multiplayer games because packet loss introduced too much latency.

Anarchy Online used the full TCP/IP with packet arrival verification. Consider two scenarios: (1) an Omni-Tek player runs past an enemy Clan player in *Anarchy Online*, and (2) an Omni-Tek player battles a Clan player. If the Omni-Tek player is merely running past the Clan player, the loss of one packet of data may not be significant. Well-designed games can interpolate the positions of characters, and they do not need to know the exact location of another character at every split second of time. Thus, UDP would be sufficient for situations like this. However, if the two players battle, as they may be expected to do at higher experience levels of *Anarchy Online*, a lost packet could be disastrous. If one player blasts the other with a ray gun, but the other gets no record of having been blasted, the two may wind up with different information about who killed whom.

Analyzing the actual data stream, Griwodz and Halvorsen found that *Anarchy Online* was sending very little data back and fourth, usually fewer than four small packets (about 120 bytes) per second per player. They comment that this means that UDP would not reduce latency much. They found that the round-trip delay time was typically on the order of 250 milliseconds – a quarter of a second – although not infrequently taking a full second, and in one case, data took 67 seconds to make a round trip between a player and the game server. Players call this *lag*, and it is a frequent topic of discussion in text chats of many games I have played. Many of the games have built-in latency meters, and mousing over them displays the exact time required for recent transactions, which I have seen as low as 90 milliseconds but more typically runs about 200, in my experience.

There have been many proposals to change the communication patterns in online games, for example, moving to a peer-to-peer system that avoids the need to communicate through a distant server, but they typically run into security problems. If the key variables – such as a player's wealth and weapon capabilities – are stored on a secure computer belonging to the game company, then it will be difficult for players with hacking skills to modify the data to their advantage. More complex network architectures have also been proposed, with some data located on local servers, and some at central points (Aggarwal et al., 2006). However, the complexity of these ideas raises its own security issues, and game companies would need to invest in creating a distributed system that had significant maintenance costs, achieving only modest reduction in latency.

Research by Pantel and Wolf (2002) suggests that latencies even as low as 50 milliseconds – one twentieth of a second – can degrade performance in real-time multiplayer games. Therefore, Bosser, A. (2004, p. 263) has argued that online games require a tradeoff between gameplay quality and the technical characteristics of Internet: "It is impossible to allow dynamic shared state to change frequently and guarantee that all hosts simultaneously access identical versions of the world." A 200 millisecond latency would be very annoying had the game designers not covered it over by the way they choreograph the action. When two players are battling, they do not usually have control over every sword thrust, and many of the actions take considerable time for the character to complete. A magical spell takes time to cast, and time to have its effect, thereby covering over the latency so the player does not perceive it. Latency would be especially problematic in melee fighting – toe to toe battles – so a variety of choreographed moves are used to hide it.

An extreme example is Boadicea, my Bear Shaman character in *Age of Conan*, a melee fighter who tends to use a sledge hammer as her weapon. This game uses *combos*, powerful attacks that require combinations of two key presses to execute. With the adjustable user interface, I have five different combos set up on the ten number keys 1 through 0. I press the 1 key to start the sequence, and then when an indicator flashes on the screen I quickly press 2 to have her start swinging the sledge hammer. Then I press 3 and wait for another indicator, when I quickly press 4. By the time I reach the 0 key, the fight may be over, but if necessary, I can return and do some of the two-key combos again, although each is available only after a significant delay. As I am doing all this, I am not really conscious of every hit that takes place in the battle, although I do often glance at the two health meters to see whether Boadicea needs to sprint away from her opponent rather than finish the fight. Boadicea constantly swings her sledgehammer, virtual blood splatters in all directions, and sometimes big red stains even cover parts of the screen as if it were a bloody window. All of these complex actions overwhelm my awareness, and Internet latency is not a factor.

In other contexts, even somewhat low latency can be highly visible. For example, a minor fad in online gaming is the use of two or more computers and avatars simultaneously, called *multi-*

boxing. I have observed a *World of Warcraft* player operate four characters simultaneously, on four computers, but my own experience is limited to two at once. Having two characters online helped me document the meetings of a scientific conference I organized inside *World of Warcraft* in May 2008 (Bohannon, J., 2008a,b) because they could take pictures at opposite ends of the group, ensure that at least one would record the text chat reliably, and perform different roles as when I had pre-programmed them to make formal announcements when I pressed a single key to run a macro. I also used two accounts, computers, and characters to analyze in some detail how pairs of characters could cooperate in action.

My best example was when Alberich the Dwarf hunter and Stephie the Gnome warlock went questing together. They would identify an enemy to attack, or a wild animal to hunt, and Alberich would move to a point just outside the distance that would have aggravated an attack. He would go into attack mode, but given the distance, this would not yet initiate the attack. Stephie would stand behind him and shoot a hostile magic spell at the target. The target would run to retaliate against her but encounter Alberich first, who without any input from me would begin slamming with his axe, bringing the enemy to a halt. I would operate Stephie, while Alberich would battle autonomously, until the enemy was dead. The strangest part of all this was what I saw on the screens of the two computers I had set up, side-by-side. The timing of events was very different on the two, things happening very noticeably earlier for the character being run from that computer, and later for the character being run on the other computer, because the two computers were connected only over a very lengthy Internet connection – a foot apart in the physical world but literally a thousand miles apart via Internet. This was most obvious if I hit both space bars simultaneously, making both characters jump. The character that belonged to one computer would have finished jumping just when the other one began.

Inspired by their study of *Starsiege*, a game designed for low-bandwidth Internet connections, Dyck et al. (2007) have outlined a number of principles for managing bandwidth and latency in games that can be usefully applied to other online purposes, such as computer supported cooperative work. Among these principles, data compression and good design are used to limit the amount of information that must be transmitted, and adaptive flow and reliability priorities are used so the system can degrade gracefully when latency rises.

Research on Internet latency can contribute to our understanding of the social dynamics in games, as a study by Suznjevic et al. (2008) illustrates. Using a software protocol analyzer named Wireshark, the team analyzed over a gigabyte of the Internet traffic on six personal computers playing *World of Warcraft*. In descending order of size of data packets, four different kinds of activity were compared: player-versus-player (PvP) combat, team raiding, completing quests, and economic trading. The effect of latency naturally depends upon the characteristics of a game and the different kinds of actions performed in it. Sheldon et al. (2003) studied the real-time strategy game *Warcraft III* and found negligible impact on the overall outcomes, but they found some hindrance specifically of exploring the game world.

3.2   SHARDING

Sharding is one of many names for dividing a virtual world into sections that are operated by different parts of a cluster of Internet servers or, at least, different parts of a single database. Small shards that are clearly demarked from the user's perspective are typically called *instances* or *dungeons*. The term *instance* implies there are two or more versions of the same section of one world running simultaneously. For example, when a team of five players enters the Sunken Temple instance in *World of Warcraft*, they will battle many monsters, but they will not encounter other players even though several teams of players may be experiencing the Sunken Temple at the same time.

Some games make very heavy use of instances, such as *Anarchy Online* and *Age of Conan*, which were launched in 2001 and 2008, respectively, by Funcom, a Norwegian company. A player who undertakes a mission in *Anarchy Online* typically needs to go into a cave or a building, which is a small instance, call it a *microinstance*. These are not tiny, and they may consist of one or two dozen rooms connected by corridors and populated by enemies, but they are simpler than the typical *World of Warcraft* instance. On occasion, the player will need to run away from several enemies, and they can even run out of the instance, where the enemies cannot follow. After regaining strength, the player can re-enter the instance and will find it about as it was before. The enemies that had been killed remain dead, but the living ones may have moved around slightly, making it easier to conquer them on a second attempt. Thus, *Anarchy Online* uses *persistent instances*, that are not automatically reset when the characters leave them, as happens in other games.

Age of Conan contains instances of many different sizes and settings. Some are truly microinstances, shops or small houses of as little as one room – even a single prison cell – where an individual player can have an experience that advances a storyline without affecting other players. Some are medium-sized, such as Conan's throne room. Other instances are very large, such as the major cities and zones of the world, each containing dozens of independent players and also containing some number of microinstances. In a few cases, the same medium-sized instance is presented as three different ones with different names because they are visited by players belonging to different nations who access it from different zones. At the moment of entering a medium-sized instance or an entire zone, players may get the option to experience it as "normal," in which the enemies are weak or "epic," in which they are strong.

One of the glories of *World of Warcraft* is that a high-level player can run across an entire continent, perhaps, for a full hour, without experiencing any jolting transition from one instance to another. As the character runs, a speck in the distance grows gracefully into a towering castle, and a notch on the horizon smoothly becomes a pass between mountains. Yes, a character can walk across the narrow bridge connecting Elwynn Forest with Westfall, but it is also possible to swim across the river at any point. Going into or out of a city requires navigating through a twisting passageway, and one suspects that the computer is furiously moving data around during those moments, but there is no sense of disjunction. However, the heavy instancing in *Age of Conan* does not make it inferior, but it merely emphasizes different qualities. Going from one zone to another always brings a temporary flash screen and a delay, and it can take place only at a designated portal, but this disjunction is compensated for by the ability to select the difficulty of a zone when entering it.

In a paper chiefly about how instances permit load balancing across servers and portions of the network, Lu et al. (2006, p. 2) note:

> There are two extremes when determining how to sub-divide a virtual world for the purposes of modeling player interaction (localized game play) and providing manageable consistency:
>
> • Geographic – world divided into regions at initialisation time to reflect the structure of a virtual world.
>
> • Behavioral – virtual world sub-divided to reflect the interaction patterns of players.

The highest level of sharding, practiced by most games, involves running multiple versions of the entire world on different sets of servers, limiting a given character to only one. In my research on *World of Warcraft*, I ran multiple characters on fully six servers, or *realms* as they are called. Some of these were identical except for whatever characters were on them, and they are used to reduce the load and thus the latency from any one of them. I have often employed the CensusPlus add-on software to do a census of all characters currently in a given realm, finding that as many as 10,000 might visit the realm during a busy day, but no more than 4,000 would be on it at once. Indeed, on several occasions, a server was so busy there was a waiting queue – and during the 2008 Lich King expansion, I once saw that 1,000 characters were waiting as long as an hour to get in – and one day, a census done right after I got in, confirmed the 4,000 maximum population.

Having multiple instances of a game, generally, means that some players cannot interact with some others. Very commonly, popular multiplayer games place servers physically in different real-world geographic locations, to serve players who live there with better connectivity (Beskow et al., 2008), and even have a gametime clock that matches local time. Often, servers in different countries employ different subscription systems as well, which means, for example, that *World of Warcraft Players* in China, North America, and Europe usually cannot play with each other. On occasion, a *World of Warcraft* realm will fill up and not permit any new players to enter it. At this point, the Blizzard company that operates the game usually advertises free transfers from that realm to specific others that are under-populated, while normally, it charges $25 to transfer a character. This can present both opportunities and challenges to groups of players, who may find it difficult to coordinate their decisions about moving in the short period of a few days when transfer is free.

A few games avoid this problem by dividing their world up in a way that does not separate some players from others. A good example is *EVE Online*, which is set in outer space and where travel from one solar system to another takes place through teleportation. All the players are on the same cluster of servers, distributed by which solar systems they happen to be in at the moment, but they are, potentially, all capable of interacting. On rare occasions, I ran into a very brief waiting queue getting into *EVE Online* when the number of players currently online exceeded something above 35,000.

3.3   GRAPHICS

This is not the place for a complete survey of computer graphics, which is a very complex field possessing many thousands of scientific publications. Our goal is to note a few of the technical aspects of graphics in online multiplayer games that have consequences for people's experience of the game and that interact in interesting ways with other topics considered here. The primary manner in which users experience virtual worlds is visually, and a successful game must give the player a solid sense of being in a particular place (Browning et al., 2006).

The key concept in understanding game graphics is that there are really two virtual environments, not one (Bainbridge and Bainbridge, 2007b). First, there is the *display model* that the user sees and which is the result of the graphics aspects of the software and data. Second, there is the *world model* that the character experiences when moving and otherwise interacting with virtual objects. For example, with respect to the display model, a wall is the surface the user sees, which will appear quite differently from different angles. The world model of a wall establishes the fact that the character cannot walk through it. Sometimes, these two models are generated by very different parts of the program or database, and there may be considerable discrepancies between them. In the display model, a wall may include a window plus niches and sculpture that realistically change appearance as the character walks past, yet the world model may depict the same wall merely as a plane that may not even be at exactly the identical apparent location as the graphically displayed wall. Sometimes the discrepancy is so great that there is an unintended gap in the world model that allows a character to walk through a wall and get into an area the game designers did not anticipate would be reachable.

Depending upon how the virtual environment is programmed, both models may impose significant demands on the user's computer. For example, if there are several non-player enemies inside a castle, they also should not be able to walk through the walls, even as they may pursue the player through the twists and turns of the hallways. A common solution is to have the world model be simpler than the display model, although there are, of course, different ways the designers can trade off computer work between the two. Ideally, the discrepancies should be at a minimum, but this is hard to achieve consistently.

A striking example is how *Entropia Universe* handles plant life, in comparison with buildings. The plants on the planet Calypso are large, colorful, and exotic, some looking very much like terrestrial moss magnified to hundreds of times its earthly size. However, all the original plants existed only in the display model, and they did not exist in the world model. That is, one's avatar could easily walk through them, whereas the wall of a building felt solid. In August 2009, when the planet was entirely recreated to accommodate a more advanced graphics engine, some new trees appeared solid, existing in both models, whereas many of the old plants remained insubstantial and did not exist in the world model.

A very difficult graphics issue that affects players is the problem of the user's viewpoint when the character is inside a building. Humans in the physical world do not have this problem because our viewpoint is set by nature to be at the location of our eyes. However, users of virtual worlds, typically, set the viewpoint above and behind the character, often a considerable distance from the eyes. This means that the point of view of the player could be obstructed by walls and other features of the architecture. Different games handle this differently. *Matrix Online* had considerable trouble, both because its rooms and corridors tended to be small, and because the graphics system would compensate unpredictably, making the image bounce around and causing difficulty moving quickly when the character was in a fight. Many other games have similar problems on staircases or other narrow spaces where the character must turn along a complex path. More than a few times one of my characters has fallen to its death because I could not tell where on a staircase or battlement it was standing.

By definition, *first-person shooter* games (such as *Chronicles of Riddick*) make the user look through the eyes of the character, for example, sighting along the barrel of a rifle toward the enemies and showing only the hands of the character or sometimes a shadow. Of the examples discussed here, *Tabula Rasa* was designed to be used either with a first-person shooter interface, or a role-playing interface, complete with different key mapping schemes, but several others permit shifting the viewpoint. Many players, especially inexperienced ones, have difficulty orienting themselves in a *first-person* view because they lack many of the other sensory cues people ordinarily experience in the real world, such as a physical sense of orientation and movement, and the peripheral vision that often lets us know where our comrades or the exits are. Therefore, most multiplayer games encourage a *third-person* view, which has the advantage of giving the person more warning when an enemy attacks from behind. To compensate, rooms inside buildings are made unnaturally large, just as the rooms in the houses depicted in television situation comedies have exaggerated dimensions.

Expert players may become accustomed to both first-person and third-person viewpoints, able to switch back and forth, but games differ enough from each other that transferring this skill from one to another is far from easy. Among the more spectacular skills in *World of Warcraft*, although seldom useful in combat, is being able to run along the horizontal ropes of the numerous sailing ships. The player goes into first-person view, places the rope directly in the center of the view, and runs forward, reliably keeping the character's feet on the rope without, however, being able to see them.

Given the complexity of the virtual worlds and the needs of advanced players to handle that complexity, new players often find learning how to use the graphic user interface a daunting experience (Cornett, S., 2004). I was about 300 hours into *World of Warcraft* before I "found my zone" when I could handle the game's excellent interface intuitively, and every new game presents a new learning curve that must be climbed. A survey carried out in ten European nations of people who played four different kinds of online games showed that, indeed, there were a substantial number of "hardcore" gamers who invested from ten to over thirty hours a week, with role playing games at the high end of the distribution (Fritsch et al., 2006, 2007). Yet every hardcore gamer was once a newbie, and the population of players grows only by attracting people who initially are strangers in a strange land.

How the graphics displayed on the screen integrate with other modalities has significant implications for user experience. For example, a group conversation in the real world is facilitated by the fact that people can see who is talking, without needing first to learn how to recognize each person's voice. As Halloran et al. (2004) have shown, the absence of visual cues can impede cooperation when a voice channel is used in online games, and adding a visual cue can be advantageous, as was done in the racing game *Midtown Madness*. Moore et al. (2007) have analyzed communications in several virtual worlds – including *EverQuest*, *Star Wars Galaxies*, and *World of Warcraft*. In addition to obvious details like the difficulty of making a character point or look in the desired direction, they noted more subtle issues such as the fact that online game text chat messages are not sent until they are finished, whereas a verbal communication in the real world is heard and responded to long before it is complete.

I have organized formal group meetings in *Second Life*, and a green indicator appears over the head of the avatar of the speaker. This has the added advantage of indicating whose microphone was inadvertently left open after speaking (responsible for annoying feedback of what somebody else is saying, for those whose sound systems do not have good methods for preventing feedback). Visual cues of who is speaking require that the voice system be integrated into the game, but even after voice was added to *World of Warcraft*, many players preferred to talk over separate systems using Skype, TeamSpeak, or Ventrillo.

Similarly, non-vocal sound effects supplement visual cues, but they are less well integrated with them than in the real world. Jørgensen, K. (2008) studied how sound effects functioned during group combat in *World of Warcraft*, especially noting the ambiguities of the meaning of sounds in complex environments. When a character goes into invisible stealth mode, a distinctive sound is heard, but it does not tell the player whether an enemy or friend has just stealthed, and thus whether to worry or be reassured. Similarly, the sound when one character casts an enhancing *buff* on a friend may have different meanings depending upon the context: "It may be a responsive signal that confirms an avatar's casting of the buff; it may identify a change in avatar state; and it may orient that avatar with respect to other avatars." Jørgensen also documents in some detail how the sound effects successfully add information to what is seen on the screen, for example, confirming whether a magical spell worked or not.

A very important dimension of the virtual environment is its architecture. The more advanced the graphics technology is, the more complex the buildings can be. Actually, there are two kinds of complexity. First, there are the graphic textures displayed on surfaces, such as the grainy appearance of individual stones in the wall of a castle. In cases where a game demands much from the user's computer, but the user's computer is only barely up to the task, the textures of somewhat distant objects may often be degraded, and they show their full granularity only from close virtual distances. Second, there is the complexity of structures experienced as the user interacts with them, for example climbing the stairs inside a castle and entering its rooms. Although graphics constrains the gameplay, the reverse is also true because good graphics must be designed to fit the nature of the game.

McGregor, G. (2006) offered evidence on this point in a study that compared the role-playing game *World of Warcraft* with the real-time strategy game *Lord of the Rings: Battle for Middle Earth 2*. Multiplayer role-playing games typically represent the user as a single avatar, through which the user experiences the world, requiring that the avatar be able to go inside buildings, caverns, and even swim through water. In a strategy game, the user often manipulates many characters at once and, even when working with a single character, operates it at a distance, emotionally as well as visually. Indeed, strategy games are sometimes called *God games* because the player operates from a lofty, almost Olympian perspective. Thus, it is not surprising that the architectural structures in *Lord of the Rings: Battle for Middle Earth 2* cannot be entered, although McGregor complains that this greatly reduces their aesthetic value. McGregor also notes that the game's large complexes of buildings often seem very strange, compared with *World of Warcraft* because they are devoid of people. Nothing quite compares with the visual excitement of the trade district of Stormwind City in *World of Warcraft*, where there are often fifty avatars rushing around in different directions, in addition to a dozen non-player characters.

Perhaps, the ultimate in realism – or in paradox – in several of the games are the bathrooms. I don't happen to know of any examples in which the characters actually need to relieve themselves in bathrooms, although they often need to eat food and drink liquids, but the bathrooms in *Matrix Online* were actually useful. Figure 3.1 shows my character, Cosmic Engineer, in the men's room on an upper floor of an office building, which he reached by riding in an elevator. His mission was to kill research subjects in a vile experiment, which accelerated the speed of the algorithms that operated them to an alarming degree, but none of them were found going to the bathroom. Indeed, the bathrooms tended to be private places where one could escape enemies. Often, Cosmic Engineer would battle too many enemies at once to defeat them all, so he would kill one, then run away to regain his lost health. A restroom was a good place to rest.

Notice that the bathroom in the picture really is a men's room; the ladies' rooms do not have stand-up urinals. When a character needs to rest and recover health, sitting down speeds up the process, and sitting on a toilet serves perfectly well. Indeed, intrepid ethnographic researcher that he was, Cosmic Engineer tried this in ladies' rooms as well, and found they did not discriminate against him on the basis of his virtual gender. Some other games have bathrooms, such as *Anarchy Online* and *Tabula Rasa*. Given that *Tabula Rasa* is a science fiction game, it was interesting to see that future technology had dispensed with toilet paper. Some of the toilets could be flushed, and when they did the water gushed upward, presumably to clean off the astronaut's posterior.

Around the edges of Figure 3.1 are the elements of the graphic user interface, which is complex in each of the popular games, but it is different in detail from one to another. At the top center are two bars of icons used to control the character during battle, with the option of scrolling to other bars that have the skill controls he uses when crafting virtual goods. In the upper right corner is the display of his status, which as in many other games is represented by a colored bar graph, here with three bars. The top (red bar) represents health which warns when death approaches. The second (yellow) bar represents the "inner strength" used to power many actions. The third (blue) bar represents the

Figure 3.1: An Office Building Men's Room in *The Matrix Online*.

growth of experience indicating one tenth of a level with blue dots below it to indicate how many tenths had been achieved. The number 34 in this display box indicates that Cosmic Engineer has reached level 34 of 50 at this point in his career.

In the lower right corner, Cosmic Engineer has set his map, which could be changed in shape to meet his momentary needs, and there is also an atlas of the entire city he could consult. The map tells him he is in the Vauxton neighborhood of the high-status Downtown part of the city, an area undergoing urban renewal. The atlas and other *Matrix* lore tell him that the residents of this section have an inferiority complex with respect to the very highest-status districts, like Creston Heights and Stratford Campus, and they scorn the merely middle-class area they call South Vauxton.

Architecture expresses social status, as the atlas recognizes: "Vauxton is usually called 'The Vox' by local residents, and anyone who calls it Vauxton is immediately tagged as an outsider."

"Unbeknownst to the South Vauxton residents struggling to get the acknowledgement they crave, the move to separate South Vauxton from Vauxton is secretly financed and backed by the business leaders of Vauxton who'd rather be rid of the undesirable south end."

On a more practical level, the map tells Cosmic Engineer where he is in the city, and he frequently consults the map, the atlas, and external online sources when he is seeking a resource or a specific destination. The display tells him his current coordinates are: X: -954 Y: 225 Z: -339. The X coordinate is how far east of the center of the Downtown he is, and it is negative, so he is on the west side. The Z coordinate is how far north he is, and it is negative, so he is slightly south of the center of the district. The Y coordinate is how high about ground level he is, and it is positive because he is in a tall office building. Each game has a different coordinate system, so switching from one to another can be confusing. For example, in *Dark Age of Camelot* the numbers can reach 50,000, because each unit equals an inch, and the numbers start at 0,0 in the northwest corner of the zone and increase eastward and southward, rather than being measured from the center as here.

The image in the map shows Cosmic Engineer where he is on the particular floor of the building, in a small room off a hallway not far from the elevator. Elevators are another good place to hide from enemies, so it is wise to keep conscious of where they are. The map does not show where the doorways are, but two different shades of red distinguish rooms he has already visited, and perhaps cleared of enemies, from those he has not yet entered. Icons sometimes locate mission goals, likely enemy locations, and locked doors for which keys must be found. Outdoors, such icons indicate mission contacts, parks, monuments, nightclubs, vendors, and the hardline telephone booths used for teleportation. The bottom center of the screen shows a compass that tells him which direction he is facing, flanked by buttons that can open up many option choices such as the atlas.

To the left of center, on the bottom, is the control panel he uses for his simulacrum, a secondary avatar not shown in this picture because he is another room resting after killing an enemy. In this case, the secondary avatar is a submachine gun bodyguard who helps fight enemies, but whom Cosmic Engineer is quite ready to sacrifice when his own life is in danger.

The lower left-hand corner of the display normally holds the multi-facetted text chat interface, but at the moment, it shows only the immediate mission objective: "Kill all of the test subjects." At certain points in the mission, a communication window opens at the lower center of the screen, giving the player orders and information, and when working with a team of other players, the text chat area can become very cluttered. The faint rectangle at the upper left corner stands where the status of an enemy would appear during a fight, but, currently, it merely contains the word "door," because the last thing Cosmic Engineer interacted with was the door to the men's room.

This picture of a bathroom illustrates the complex relationship between the virtual world and real world, including the great complexity of a graphic user interface that must be learned well before it can be used well. In the three *Matrix* movies, users jacked into the system through a direct brain interface at the base of their skulls, and they were not conscious that the world they interacted with was inside a computer. Many researchers still hope to develop fully immersive virtual reality in which the user acts in the normal manner by moving legs and arms and hands and fingers.

But at the present time, cumbersome user interfaces interact with increasingly realistic but still obviously artificial graphic virtual worlds. Much of the psychological feeling of immersion comes from emotional engagement with the lore, the quests, and the online social groups. At the same time, the graphic display, including the user interface, is part of a system that controls human behavior even as it liberates human fantasies.

CHAPTER 4

Rolecoding and Social Control

Rolecoding is connected to security, privacy, access control, group membership and role playing. It refers to rules built into the game, rather than enforced through persuasion or punishment, that control the ways in which particular characters can interact with each other. The social roles of online game characters, and thus of their players, are sharply defined in many ways. For example, my *Anarchy Online* character, Nanobic, is an engineer working for the Omni-Tek Corporation. Figure 4.1 shows him sharing Christmas with his robot friend, Tobor.

Figure 4.1: Nanobic and Tobor Celebrating in *Anarchy Online*.

Most other kinds of AO characters cannot create and control robots, and most games described here strictly impose a division of labor upon characters and thus upon players. One could argue, without too much exaggeration, that the rules of the game constrain Nanobic as much as Tobor and thus that the player is transformed into a kind of robot as well. The player's chief options are which game to subscribe to, and what kind of character to select from a pre-defined set.

4.1   SYSTEMS OF RULES

Given that much of the action in online games involves "killing" other characters, some of whom are operated by other players, and stealing virtual goods from them, it is hard to say what the basis of morality could be. Some rules are written into the user agreements that every player must accept, others are programmed into the code as firm technical barriers against certain kinds of behavior, and others are informally adopted by groups of players within these virtual worlds. What are we to make, both technically and ethically of the following case described by Craft, A. (2007, p. 205)?

> On April 18, 2005 Istvaan Shogaatsu, the leader of a group of mercenaries called the Guiding Hand Social Club in *EVE Online*, announced that his organization had just completed one of the biggest acts of theft and betrayal in the history of virtual worlds. Members of the Guiding Hand spent a year infiltrating a rival organization before assassinating their leader and stealing in-game assets valued at 16,500 US dollars, effectively shattering the trust within the organization's social network setting its members back months of playing time.

Several games make a distinction between servers where player-versus-player (PvP) combat is encouraged, and those where both players must agree to have a duel before one can attack the other. Thus, the populations of players differ across them, with more aggressive players choosing the PvP realms. In *EVE Online*, which emphasizes PvP play for advanced players, much of the galaxy is wide open, but a few hundred solar systems have a security force which deters one player from attacking another. It is very common for PvP games to suppress PvP in the areas for starting players or otherwise vary the constraints from one area to another. A few *World of Warcraft* realms are designated for role playing (RP), suggesting but not requiring that players stay in character. I even saw one example in which a guild of players had two text chat channels, one for RP communications and one for talk about the players' "real world" lives.

Building the rules into the game, so that it is impossible to violate them, is a cost-effective solution from the standpoint of game designers. For example, in many games when one player agrees to buy something from another, a trade window opens up, and the exchange does not complete until both players click buttons indicating they agree. Thus, there is no possibility for one player to steal from another. However, if one player agrees to perform a service for another, there may be no practical way to build a safety mechanism into the code of the game, to ensure that the money does not get paid until the service has been performed, and that the money will indeed be paid after satisfactory service.

The typical solution to this problem of trust is to build into the game a system for managing groups of players, like the guilds in *World of Warcraft*. Each guild is founded by a guild master, who can set the rules of access to the guild management system by members of different ranks – for example, specifying which categories of members can recruit new members and expel existing members. If one member abuses the trust of others, the victims can talk with an officer of the guild, who may admonish the troublesome member, or may even boot him or her from the guild. Most recent games that have such player organizations incorporate rather complex management systems that allow the leaders of the guild to make a range of decisions about such things as how many ranks their group will have and what privileges each rank will enjoy.

A guild master in *World of Warcraft*, as I learned with the three guilds I myself ran, has a guild control window in the user interface where such rules can be set. Several relate to communication permissions. Can members of the given rank speak and/or listen in the guild chat and in a chat reserved for officers of the guild? Do they have the power to set the guild's "message of the day" that appears in the text chat whenever a player logs into the character? In the guild part of the social module in the user interface, any member can see a list of the guild members, including whether or not they are currently online and what zone of the virtual world they are in. Also accessible is a window displaying any information a fellow guild member wants to post about the character, called a *public note*. Officers of the guild can also place an *officer note* there, which may not be visible to the player who owns the character, and might be critical of the player. Thus, three permissions the guild master may give high ranking members is editing a player's public note and seeing or editing the officer note.

Of course, important powers are inviting new people to join the guild, removing inactive or troublesome members from the guild, and promoting or demoting up and down the ladder of ranks. Many guilds allow all but the very lowest, provisional rank of membership is to recruit new members, but reserve promotions, demotions and removals are for officers to handle. Often, one sees automatic announcements of these changes in the guild chat. When a new person joins, that player gains access to the guild chat, which announces by name the character has just joined. The members who are online exclaim "welcome," and some immediately offer advice to the newcomer. Often, a barrage of messages announces a series of promotions, and people share congratulations. At the middle ranks, promotions tend to depend simply upon being an active member and not causing trouble. The guild part of the interface provides information on when a character was last online, and some guilds regularly demote those who have not played within the past month, and expel members who have been absent for a long time, although practices in this area vary widely. Expulsions and voluntary defections by members are also automatically announced in the chat, and they frequently provoke discussion.

Some of the largest or best-organized guilds conduct a fair amount of their business on websites and through private forums that require a player to register and seek permissions, and these are also used to screen new recruits. Thus, part of the rolecoding takes place outside the game itself, in these web-based social computing sites operated by guilds or comparable groups associated with one game or another.

The *World of Warcraft* guild-master module also provides control over the guild bank or vault, which itself is accessed only at banks in major cities in the virtual world. There, characters may contribute virtual money or goods of various kinds, such as armor they do not need themselves, or useful virtual objects they have crafted using specialized professional skills. The guild master can decide whether a given rank has any access to the guild bank at all, and only those with permission can donate items or even see how much is already there. Some guilds allow only officers to withdraw items or money, and this gives them a nice social function in distributing those valuables among needy members. But the guild master can follow any policy in giving a rank the ability to withdraw, including setting limits on how much can be taken in a single day.

4.2   DEVIANT BEHAVIOR

If some rules are programmed into the game mechanics, while others are a matter of customary behavior of players, what are the boundaries of the concept *cheating*, and how can different forms of it be controlled? Perhaps the most blatant form involves using special software or hardware to change the data of a game, to favor the user. This is common with solo-player games, and many people use GameShark hardware or software, feeling it is not cheating because in solo play no other player is put at a disadvantage by the use of GameShark. Of course, once people share the results of their solo play – "I just finished Game X in record time!" – a competitive element enters the ethical equation.

Online multi-player games typically prevent this kind of cheating by keeping a secure centralized database containing all competition-relevant statistics for each player. To reduce latency and cost, game developers might want to move to a peer-to-peer system, and, indeed, peer-to-peer is often used for handling updates of game content, but not of actual gameplay. With the goal of ultimately designing cheat-proof peer-to-peer systems, Webb and Soh (2007); cf. Li et al. (2004) drew upon earlier researchers to develop a typology of cheats. Peer-to-peer systems are especially vulnerable because many of these cheats involve transmitting wrong information that may have significant impact upon competition even if the central controller of the peer-to-peer network seeks periodically to synchronize information across all players. Invalid commands can be sent or inconsistency across players is created by sending different updates to different people. Suppressed update, timestamp, and replay cheats alter the time at which information is sent. In spoofing, one player masquerades as another. Webb and Soh define five other kinds of cheats that are more subtle and can be carried out with central server games that lack the vulnerabilities of peer-to-peer, so I shall expand upon their analysis of those types here.

Exploit is the common gaming term for exploiting a bug or other weakness in a game, and a few of the games actually prohibit exploits in their user agreements. Many advanced players, however, consider exploits to be the highest form of play, deserving more honor than mere obedience to the rules. The most powerful expression of this viewpoint was offered by Robinett, W. (2003) who did essentially this when he programmed the very first easter egg into the computer game *Adventure* way back in 1978. *Easter egg* is the term for a valuable item that is hidden somewhere in the virtual environment and can be used to do something unusual. The game company Robinett was working for, Atari, did not want its game creator's names to be publicized, but he felt he deserved recognition for this pioneering effort. Therefore, he placed a gray dot at one point in a maze, which was the key to a secret room accessible at another point, in which "Warren Robinett" would flash on the screen in rainbow colors. As game designer, Robinett was playing a *metagame* with the company and with the ordinary players. Exploits are a way in which players can win a metagame against the companies and designers as well as the ordinary players who lack the knowledge or the motivation to take the game to a higher level.

An example of a type of exploit requiring two or more players was offered by Wright et al. (2002), who studied the early online first-person shooter game, *Counter-Strike*. Typically, two teams of commandos are fighting in a complex but well-defined territory. Characters who are killed do not immediately come back to life, so their players are allowed to observe events but not participate in them, even shifting the location from which their ghosts were observing. To prevent dead players from functioning as spies, they are blocked from using the usual in-game chat communications system. However, some players discovered they could still communicate through a subsidiary channel, so they could scout out the enemy deployment and report back to the still-living members of their team. This exploit is called *ghosting*, and is considered here as an exploit rather than placing it in the collusion category (below), because it depends upon a technical vulnerability of the system, but it also could be described as an espionage hack.

Espionage hacks are actions based on special technical knowledge that give the player information he is not entitled to have. As Cikic et al. (2008) note, "Quite a few cheats actually revolve around knowing things that the player is not supposed to know (yet). Famous examples are the well-known maphacks and wallhacks, where the player sees what happens in areas he cannot currently see, or has not ever seen. These cheats are some of the hardest to detect, prevent, and prosecute, as even a total replay of the situation, with all possible data available, will often not prove that the player cheated, he may just have guessed well." Although some of these cases involve running software that lets the player see from a different location than the game itself would provide, many of the ones that are possible today are exploits more than hacks.

The general response from game developers is to level the playing field, sometimes achieving an advantage for themselves in so doing, and the response from players has been to share the knowledge so widely that it ceases to confer an advantage. For example, in *World of Warcraft*, a player cannot see sections of a map of the territory unless that player's character has already visited those sections. The map starts largely blank, and it fills in only step by step as the character legitimately acquires information about each section. Typically, the full map is already on the player's computer, hidden among the graphics files, and could be located and decoded, given sufficient computing skill, what is called a *maphack*. However, once players had visited all parts of a map, they could take a screenshot of it and post it on their websites, so every new player would have access. Blizzard Entertainment, the company that produces *World of Warcraft*, did them one better, printing all the maps in a series of atlases, along with additional charming drawings of each and every small town in its vast virtual world.

Wallhacks are exploits that allow a player to see through a supposedly opaque wall – or to reach through a supposedly solid wall – and often depend on a local flaw in the game's database. For example, when I first started playing *World of Warcraft*, wallhacks could be done on two sunken ships. To legitimately reach the objectives in these two ships, a character had to swim down into the water and battle obnoxious amphibians called murlocs, all the while holding a virtual breath. Several dives were necessary, and if the character were "killed," there would be time for the dead murlocs to respawn so the battle would start all over from the beginning. However, it was possible to swim down outside each ship, to a certain point in the stern, and grab the quest object through the solid wall. After a few months, this vulnerability was closed, and the wallhack no longer worked. As with many other kinds of exploit, the ultimate cure is adding preventive measures to the game code, rather than punishing offenders.

Given that cooperation among players is an important part of many online games, they offer a range of groupware technologies to manage raiding parties, long-lived guilds, and permanent category divisions such as combat factions. What Webb and Soh (2007) call *collusion* is cooperation between players who are nominally in competing groups. I reported a remarkable sequence of collusion and counter-collusion in my book about *World of Warcraft* (Bainbridge, W., 2010c, p. 136–137) It is possible for a player to have both Horde and Alliance characters in the same realm, as I myself did, and the following incident was observed by Etacarinae from the Alliance side, and Incognita from the Horde side. The only collusion between them concerned placing them at the right spots to collect data, but I could just as easily have used collusion between them to influence events.

Etacarinae was going about some ordinary business in Stormwind, the Human city, when a rumor came over the local Alliance text chat that the Horde was about to attack. Presumably, a player was using a Horde character as a spy and passing the information to the Alliance through a second Alliance character. Etacarinae and several others ran to the front gate of the city, ready to block entry. They grew restless as the minutes passed without incident; then, a second message said that the Horde raiding party was crossing the bridge from Westfall. Thinking to cut off the Horde advance at that point, the defenders rushed to the bridge but saw no invaders. Rushing back to Stormwind, they discovered they had been tricked, and the Horde raiders had penetrated deep into the city before being killed. Probably, it had all been a trick. A player loyal to the Horde had used an Alliance character to lure the Alliance players first to the main gate and then over to the bridge, leaving the entrance undefended.

When the attack was over, Etacarinae's guild began organizing a retaliation. Because guild members have some basis of trust, it is relatively safe for them to plan attacks using the text chat that is reserved for members. The player who tricked the Stormwind defenders did not need to belong to a guild and, indeed, could have created an Alliance character only minutes before for the sole purpose of placing disinformation in the local Alliance chat. The guild decided to attack Orgrimmar, one of the Horde cities, which required long distance travel. Travel takes time, and it reveals intentions, because one of the non-guild Alliance characters could have been the Horde spy. I switched over to my Horde character, Incognita, and I headed for Orgrimmar. Word came over the Horde chat that the Alliance was planning an attack on a different Horde city, Silvermoon. This, I knew, was disinformation. The obvious attack point on Orgrimmar is the main gate on the south side, but the Alliance planned to attack the west gate, instead, so that was where I placed Incognita. This retaliatory attack was less successful than the original, but both included disinformation communicated by means of collusion between characters nominally belonging to opposed factions. On several other occasions when one of my characters participated in raiding by a well-organized guild, the leadership did not announce the target until they were very close, and they chose routes that disguised their destination.

Cheating is not the only crime in virtual worlds, and among the most prominent other offenses is *griefing*, taking pleasure from causing harm to other players. Foo and Koivisto (2004) have suggested there are four distinguishable types of griefing. *Harassment* annoys other players through shouting slurs in the text or voice chat, spamming a channel repeatedly, placing one's avatar in the way of the other player's avatar, and disrupting events. *Power imposition* is more violent, often consisting of repeatedly killing a weaker player. *Scamming* involves such misdeeds as breaking promises and deceiving other players about one's identity. *Greed play* is like stealing, for example, *ninja looting* by taking the loot from a dead non-player character that rightfully belongs to another player, or *kill stealing* that joins a fight at the last moment hoping to get credit for the kill.

Rolecoding systems in some games effectively prevent some but not all of these behaviors. For example, many text chat systems have an ignore command that forever prevents a spammer from sending you a message, and many games assign loot and kill credit to the first player who attacked the enemy, thereby preventing ninja looting and kill stealing. Rolecoding affects groups as well as individuals. For example, team quests and instances are designed for a certain number of players, require the exercise of a particular combination of skills for success, and provide standardized methods of communication between players while they are on the team (Bardzell et al., 2008; Chen et al., 2008).

Barnett et al. (2010) carried out a questionnaire study to determine what made players angry at other players in *World of Warcraft*. Griefing and harassment were among the four factors they found, but two others that proved very important have not been studied extensively in previous work. Most anger-causing scenarios involve the failure of one player to live up to the expectations of another, notably in raids or instances where teamwork is essential, and other scenarios concern simple time-wasting. Interestingly, feeling angry did not depend on believing that the other player intentionally misbehaved. This may suggest a blind area in prior research, because while there has been much discussion of intentional norm-violation, there has been little about incompetence.

4.3   GAME MASTERS AND MENTORS

Online roleplaying games are an outgrowth of old-style pencil and paper roleplaying games, including tabletop games using cards or dice exemplified by *Dungeons and Dragons* released in 1974. Even earlier, the 1949 board game *Cluedo* (called *Clue* in North America) had players take different roles in a murder mystery. The rules of *Cluedo* were unambiguous, and each time the game was played one of the characters selected by the drawing of a card would be secretly assigned guilt for the murder. Thus, as with other popular board games, any reasonable set of people could understand and follow the written rules. *Dungeons and Dragons* was complex, and it permitted considerable elaborations, so it required one person to take the role of *game master*. As the current Wikipedia article for the game says, "A Dungeon Master serves as the game's referee and storyteller, while also maintaining the setting in which the adventures occur"[1]. When roleplaying games were created online, many of the former functions of the game master were encoded into the software, but a few functions remained that human beings had to perform.

With the role of game master in mind, Tychsen, A. (2006); Tychsen et al. (2005) says that role-playing games have five common features. First, these games are "storytelling with rules," which implies that someone or something must perform the storytelling function. Second, the players operate characters inside the fictional reality, through which they interact. Third, each particular game reality rests upon a unique premise: "This is a shared understanding among the game participants of the game setting, the starting point of the game, the rules and similar framework properties" (Tychsen, A., 2006, p. 76). Fourth, these games are usually guided either by a human game master, or, in the case of many electronic games, by the game engine. Fifth, role-playing games like those considered here require at least two people – often many – one of whom may be the game master.

One distinction across games of many kinds is whether the game master can also be a player. The banker in *Monopoly*, for example, is in no position to cheat, so being banker does not confer an advantage that prevents the banker from also playing. Massively multiplayer online games would probably never be profitable if all the traditional game master functions were performed by employees of the game company, but not all of these functions can be automated. Thus, some game master functions may be given to the players, while a few are reserved for employees.

One of the functions of the traditional game master is educational, teaching new players and guiding more experienced players to achieve a satisfying play experience. MMORPGs, generally, do this automatically, by establishing special areas of the virtual world for newcomers and giving them a set of beginner missions that teach them about both the game mechanics and the fictional premise. Both *Tale in the Desert* and *Age of Conan* place newcomers on an island, which they cannot leave until they have completed their training. In the case of *Tale in the Desert*, the training emphasizes technology, for example, how to make stone blades from slate and use them to cut boards from wood taken from the trees. In *Age of Conan*, the player learns the mythos about how Conan's arch enemy, the Stygian sorcerer Thoth-Amon, is preparing a magical army to attack Aquilonia, and he learns how civilization is threatened by wild tribes along all of its borders as this major war brews. Many games use *delivery quests* to teach players about the virtual world's geography, even at very advanced experience levels, sending the player by land, sea or air to distant locations, supposedly

---

[1] http://en.wikipedia.org/wiki/Dungeons_and_Dragons

to give supplies or information to a remote ally, but, actually, to make the player familiar with the destination.

Entropia Universe handles training very differently. It offers no explicit quests or missions although the rich environment of the planet Calypso suggests many reasons a player might want to explore. Rather it urges each new player to select a human mentor, a role taken by more experienced players, who will help the newbie identify personal goals and the means to achieve them. When I entered *Entropia Universe*, I decided that my research would work better if I did not seek a mentor inside the world, and I used a variety of web-based sources instead. However, one of those resources was a very fine book-length guide written by one of the mentors, using the name Alice in Wonderland[2].

A second function of game masters, which overlaps the first, is to help players solve problems. In rare cases, these may involve data corruption or bugs where only an employee of the game company has the power to help. *Entropia Universe* provides a fascinating example of a serious problem experienced by some players and solved by others, which I myself experienced. I had set myself the goal of reaching all of the teleporters which provide easy transit from place to place, but as with many games, each one must be reached on foot before it is added to the player's list of useable teleporters. With just four left to go, I got totally stuck at a resurrection station in an advanced zone, which was surrounded by vicious monsters. I tried many times to sneak out, but I was repeatedly killed and resurrected back at the station. I sought help from the Calypso Rescue Team, an organization of helpful players, and two of them quickly came to lead me out, one killing the monsters and the other healing him from their damage[3].

Age of Conan has an organization, called the Followers of Asura, who are player volunteers who help other players and also assist the development team find and fix bugs. To add drama to their work, they are described as a mystical secret society: "The history of the Followers is shrouded in mystery. Little is known about their actions or motivations, but tales of their knowledge and assistance are legend. The Followers have come to the aid of many a Hyborian in times of need, even King Conan himself"[4]. One of the more established medieval fantasies, *Dark Age of Camelot*, has a similar program in which volunteers work with Mythic company employees to share game master duties:

> The goal of the Knights of the Round Table program is to harness the knowledge and experience of the customer base to assist the developers in ensuring that Camelot remains stable, balanced, and fun to play. The Knights are players who volunteer their free time to assist the Dark Age of Camelot development team by acting as a conduit between Mythic and the larger player community, providing feedback and testing of upcoming changes, and suggesting new ideas on ways to improve Camelot. Each Knight has an

[2] http://rp.apachenet.de/downloads/Entropia_Guide.pdf
[3] http://v2.euforces.com/
[4] http://cs.ageofconan.com/Public/

area of responsibility. Some Knights are advocates for their realm while others speak on behalf of the citizens of all realms and the game, at large[5].

4.4   LEGAL REGIME

With *EverQuest* as his example, Lastowka, G. (2009) suggests that the legal regulation of an online game has three distinct frameworks. First, as fictive text a game is a work of art, belonging to the company that created it, and regulated by intellectual property law. This categorization is somewhat problematic, because it leaves open the question of to what extent the players are also creators, and where the line should be drawn between the intellectual property of the company and that of the players. Second, as a computer game *EverQuest* has rules, and many of these rules are built into the programming codes so that players cannot violate them. This contrasts with ordinary games, in which the rules are enforced by the players themselves or in some cases by referees, and raises the question of how online games would define and enforce rules if they were not built into the code. Third, as an online community, *EverQuest* could have norms above and beyond those written into the code, but this raises two immediate questions: is the *EverQuest* community distinct from the wider society and thus able to have its own rules? Is the *EverQuest* community unified, or is it really a set of separate communities that overlap and interact as social groups do within the game?

On Lastowka's first point, Humphreys, S. (2009) argues that the current laws and contracts give all the power to the companies hosting games and virtual worlds, without recognizing the contributions made by the players. Users cannot negotiate the user agreements with the companies and are forced to accept complex rules they may not understand. Typically, these agreements give the company the right to expel a user without granting any appeal, despite the fact that user may have invested much time advancing their characters and creating social relations. Indeed, the current legal regime does not recognize the affective and social contributions of the players, and it conceptualizes the game in an old-fashioned manner equivalent to fully-scripted works of art like novels. Humphreys suggests that hosting an online community is much more like a service than a product, and thus the wrong traditional rules are being applied.

Grimes, S. (2006) has not only laid out the intellectual property issues for games that are jointly created by companies and players, but she has argued that American law is moving rapidly toward corporate rather than community ownership of culture. She cites some specific court cases, including one involving a small Mexican gold farming sweatshop, where employees played *Dark Age of Camelot* to earn virtual currency to sell to ordinary players, something that would not seem to violate society's laws, unless society is required to enforce the user agreements games require. Dibbell, J. (2007) has explored the world of Chinese gold farmers, for whom playing *World of Warcraft* is a livelihood as well as occasionally fun. Other examples include *EverQuest's* campaign to stop people from selling virtual property on eBay. If people really "own" the items they earn in the games, then of course they should be able to sell them, but the companies argue they own the items on the basis of their intellectual property rights and user agreements. A key issue is political. If people can advance in the

---

[5] http://www.camelotherald.com/knights/

games by paying gold farmers or hiring others to advance their characters for them, then economic inequalities from the outside world infect the game, and players are no longer rewarded in terms of their skill and effort but how big their real-world bank accounts are.

CHAPTER 5

Personality and Motivation

Players bring different styles, goals, habits, values, and temperaments to their gaming; their personalities influence their behavior and thus the experiences of other players. In addition, the games are filled with non-player characters who must behave in an interesting and somewhat realistic manner; they need personalities as well in the increasingly sophisticated social environments of online games.

5.1 PSYCHOLOGICAL THEORIES AND TYPOLOGIES

Traditionally, *personality* is conceptualized in psychological terms as a persistent predisposition to feel and behave in ways characteristic for the individual (Lindzey et al., 1968). Throughout human history, people have described each other in terms like hot and cold, dominant and submissive, kind and cruel. Early in the twentieth century, psychologists began to systematize these folk concepts. An influential research method using questionnaires was pioneered by Raymond Cattell, although he himself believed that observational and experimental data were also needed. In an iterative process extending across many studies, researchers would develop a long list of questionnaire items, for example, phrases describing a person in ordinary language that expressed a range of concepts about personality. People would rate these items in terms of how well or poorly each one described themselves, or they described some particular other person they knew well. Then statistical techniques like factor analysis would be used to identify which items cluster together along what number of general dimensions of meaning. Through such methods, Cattell came up with fully 16 personality dimensions, although subsequent researchers have felt that this is too great a number and have not been able to confirm much of his research using more modern variants of his methods.

The most widely cited personality classification system is the so-called "Big-5" dimensions, which exist in somewhat different variants. The so-called OCEAN version (McCrae and Costa, 1996, p. 67) is:

1. Openness to experience: fantasy, aesthetics, feelings.

2. Conscientiousness: competence, order, dutifulness.

3. Extraversion: warmth, gregariousness, assertiveness.

4. Agreeableness: trust, straightforwardness, altruism.

5. Neuroticism: anxiety, angry hostility, depression.

This system is solidly rooted in self-report psychological assessments studies but also supported by observational studies of behavior. To be sure, there are questions about the exact meanings of these five supposedly distinct dimensions, notably about "openness to experience," which is sometimes equated with "intelligence," and cross-cultural studies show local variations as well as a degree of commonality (Yang and Bond, 1990).

Arguably the five dimensions should have implications for the behavior of a game player. Extraversion implies sociability, and characters may differ in the degree that they participate in guilds and other groups, versus solo questing in the virtual world. Both conscientiousness and agree-ableness may be valuable for cooperation with other players to achieve shared goals, and good co-workers would logically score high on these characteristics. These two dimensions also have also been connected to control of impulses that might otherwise express themselves through vio-lence (Jensen-Campbell et al., 2007; Jensen-Campbell and Malcolm, 2007), and collective violence is a major form of cooperation in games. Neuroticism might imply a disability in cooperating reliably over time with others, whereas openness to experience could encourage exploration and discovery in this virtual world as well as in the "real world."

Despite its prominence, the Big-5 model has limitations. Largely based on self-report ques-tionnaire data, backed up by some modest behavioral studies, it has two debatable features. First, it assumes that humans should be distinguished in terms of a small number of uncorrelated dimen-sions, rather than, for example, by a very large number of psychological scales that may have complex relationships to each other and are often relevant only to some people. The statistical methods used to create and validate the Big-5, such as factor analysis, are based on the dimensional assumption, and thus they do not seriously test it. Second, its empirical measures chiefly concern mild behaviors, such as those relevant to sedate psychology classrooms and college campuses. For example, rather than wondering whether conscientiousness and agreeableness inhibit violence, one might postulate a primary personality dimension measuring propensity to violence that cannot be measured accurately by the bland questionnaire items of the Big-5.

5.2   GAME-BASED THEORIES

Violence, at least in attenuated form, is central to most online games, and thus it is conceivable that a personality theory deriving from games rather than classrooms would have some advantages over the Big-5, and on average it could be no more unrealistic than those based on research inside the artificial academic world. There is at least one candidate for such a theory, the four motivations for online game playing suggested by Bartle, R. (1996, 2004):

1. Achievement within the game context (achievers).

2. Exploration of the game (explorers).

3. Socializing with others (socializers).

4. Imposition upon others (killers).

Bartle suggests that these four categories can be mapped in two dimensions: acting versus interacting and orientation toward players versus toward the world. Of those oriented toward other players, killers act and socializers interact. Of those oriented toward the virtual world, achievers act and explorers interact. But one could also connect these ideas with standard psychological concepts. Achievers might be high on need for achievement, socializers high on need for affiliation, and killers high on need for power, the three dimensions of psychologist McClelland, D. (1961) personality theory, which does not map perfectly upon the Big-5. Explorers, in contrast, could reflect openness to experience, the most ambiguous of the Big-5 dimensions.

Yee, N. (2006) has explored the motivations of players from an empirical perspective, while mindful of Bartle's theory-based concepts, using a 40-item questionnaire scale. A starting point was an open-ended question administered to player of *EverQuest*: "Why does *EverQuest* appeal to you?" Yee culled the written responses for different reasons why the game appealed to different people, and he also drew upon Bartle's publications for additional items. He then administered the motivation scale to 6,675 players of such games and performed statistical factor analysis, identifying five distinct dimensions of variation in the data. Here is how Yee defines the five most important motivational factors:

1. Relationship: "To interact with other users, and their willingness to form meaningful relationships."

2. Manipulation: "To objectify other users and manipulate them for... personal gain and satisfaction."

3. Immersion: "Being in a fantasy world... being 'someone else'."

4. Escapism: "To temporarily... escape from real-life stress and problems."

5. Achievement: "To become powerful in the context of the virtual environment."

Exploratory factor analysis often leaves a number of items either standing alone or in two-item groupings that are hard to interpret. Yee saw some evidence of three additional factors that could in principle be defined more precisely in future research that included many more similar items. One concerned how much people like to lead others, the second emphasized what people believe they learn about themselves through playing the game, and the final one distinguished people who prefer solo play versus team play.

Statistical clustering methods like factor analysis work best in identifying major dimensions of variation that relate to most people, but it is certainly possible that some motivations are highly idiosyncratic. If a motivation was salient for a tiny fraction of players but not meaningful to many others, it would not show up in factor analysis, nor might the usual methods of item creation produce measures that could detect it. However, researchers could start from a different premise and discover such motivations, and some of them might be theoretically significant.

One motivation that immediately comes to mind, but it may not yet have been studied systematically, concerns fans of the particular mythos on which a game was based. For example, *Star Wars* or *Conan* fans might not be particularly oriented toward online games, but they start playing

Star Wars Galaxies or *Age of Conan* in order to experience a continuation of the enjoyment they have felt watching the movies and reading the books. This very special motivation might correlate with Yee's immersion and escapism dimensions, but it also has a special quality we might call *cultural commitment* – valuing the distinctive qualities of a mythos, perhaps, simply from familiarity. An analogy in the real world would be nationalism. People differ in how nationalistic they are, but nationalists differ from each other in terms of which nation they value. Of course some worlds, such as *EverQuest*, were not based closely on a pre-existing mythos, and thus cultural commitment might not matter for them, or it would exist only at a high level of abstraction, for example, being a fantasy fan rather than a science fiction fan.

Yee, N. (2009) has shown that different games attract and reinforce somewhat different personality orientations, comparing *EverQuest* primarily with *World of Warcraft* but also with others. In particular, *EverQuest* seems especially capable of building strong relations of friendship and mutual aid. To begin with, people self-select by entering this somewhat mild fantasy game, which requires a good deal of patience, rather than a first person shooter or other more violent game. As people play *EverQuest*, they find that they absolutely must team up with others. Compared with *World of Warcraft*, *EverQuest* characters have more specialized abilities. For example, clerics are good at healing but lack good attack spells, whereas the equivalent class in *World of Warcraft*, priests, can acquire powerful attack spells as well as healing. Thus, characters with different strengths gain immeasurably by teaming up. In addition, the temporary death of a character is more costly in *EverQuest*, and that cost can be reduced through the help of other players. Put the other way around, *World of Warcraft* is more readily soloable than *EverQuest*. Yee believes that one consequence of *EverQuest's* natural sociability is that many online friendships become real world friendships.

Holsapple and Wu (2007) have suggested a different framework for understanding player's motivations, with seven categories: (1) fantasy daydreams, (2) role projection allowing the person to experience a new role, (3) escapism from problems and pressures in the real world, (4) enjoyment and the experience of fun, (5) emotional involvement that makes the person feel a part of the game, (6) arousal whether mere excitement or profound inspiration, and (7) behavior reflecting the probability of playing the game without attributing a specific motive.

Online games often have their own theories of personality, embodied in attributes of the character that provide more or less technical advantage under various circumstances, but which also can be interpreted in more psychological terms. A good example is *Matrix Online*, which had a system of five attribute variables which the player could build up differentially in the process of gaining experience levels: perception, focus, reason, belief, and vitality. At the very beginning when creating a character, the player must choose one of the ten personality types listed in Table 5.1, each of which has a different distribution of 40 points across the five attributes (Bedman, 2007).

Note that each of the ten types is high in one attribute, low in another, and average in the remaining three. Arguably, the five attributes are a five-factor theory of personality dimensions, competing with the Big-5 popular among academic psychologists. Some of the dimensions even seem comparable, focus with conscientiousness, and perception with openness to experience – although

Table 5.1: Point distributions across attributes and personalities in *Matrix Online*.

Personality Type	Perception (awareness of environment)	Focus (control, concentration)	Reason (problem solving)	Belief (confidence, conviction)	Vitality (physical wellbeing)
Detached Spectator	11	5	8	8	8
Devoted Ascetic	8	8	8	11	5
Fanatic Self Improver	8	8	8	5	11
Inquisitive Genius	8	8	11	5	8
Lunatic Fringe	8	8	5	11	8
New Age Hippy	8	11	5	8	8
Secluded Introvert	5	11	8	8	8
Suspicious Cynic	11	8	8	5	8
Troubled Intellectual	8	5	11	5	8
True Believer	5	8	8	11	8

the intellect interpretation of openness in the Big-5 seems closer to reason in the Matrix-5. One of the ten Matrix types, Secluded Introvert, even uses the introversion-extraversion language of one of the Big-5. Here is how the game described that type: "You never had many friends. Well, except the ones in your head. They said the world didn't need you. They had it wrong. You didn't need the world."

The true believer personality type seems to harmonize with the messianic quality of the *Matrix* mythos and the orientations of the friends of the main character in the three *Matrix* movies who come to believe he is The One who will save the world. It emphasizes conviction in one's beliefs, while minimizing awareness of anything in the environment that might challenge these beliefs. Its description in the game is: "Possible and impossible are the states of mind. Everything is not what it seems. Sometimes the senses lie. And you knew why all along." Traditionally, psychologists described true belief as an attribute of the pathological authoritarian personality (Adorno et al., 1950). Frankly, the scientific literature in that area is hard to evaluate because it grew out of analysis of fascist mentalities in the emotional wake of World War II, was developed by avowedly left-wing scholars—although some who criticized right-wing mentalities like Lipset and Raab (1970) and Bell, D. (1963) evolved from socialists into neo-conservatives during their own lives—and true belief might be considered a virtue by conservatives rather than an authoritarian vice.

5.3   THEORETICAL DEBATES

Psychologists and social scientists have developed a very large number of concepts and measurement scales to distinguish individuals in terms of their styles of thought, feeling, and behavior. Many of these concepts overlap while some are very specialized, yet potentially a large fraction could usefully be applied to players of multiplayer games and inhabitants of non-game virtual worlds. Personality concepts vary greatly in terms of how well supported they are by scientific evidence, in terms of how meaningful they are to non-scientists, and thus how useful they would be for non-technical discussions about games. Unfortunately, some widely-held theories are probably wrong, and some of the most popular psychological concepts are not based in good science.

An example is the Myers-Briggs Type Indicator, a widely used self-report questionnaire instrument that supposedly divides people into a small number of distinct types. Based on ninety-year-old ideas of Carl Jung, Sigmund Freud's most mystical prominent follower, the MBTI seems to fit what many ordinary people think about the personalities of others, but it has numerous deficiencies as a scientific instrument. First of all, it thinks in terms of types, whereas the Big-5 thinks in terms of dimensions. It may not be valid to capture the rich complexity of an individual in terms of either scheme, but typological thinking is worse than dimensional thinking because it often assigns people to separate categories on the basis of very small real differences. The MBTI was created decades ago by people who lacked advanced scientific training. It tends to get what empirical support it has from studies by practitioners who have a vested interest because they use the test in professional counseling. Studies by well-trained academics raise severe doubts about the test's overall validity, although one of Jung's concepts, extraversion, found its way into the Big-5 as well (McCrae and Costa, 1989).

While recognizing the importance of over-arching concepts like the Big-5, it is essential also to acknowledge that a school of personality research connected to the psychoanalytic tradition has examined the distinctive characteristics of individuals (Smith et al., 1956; Murray, H., 1981). Such person-oriented research is sometimes called *ideographic*, in distinction to the *nomothetic* research that seeks general principles that apply across individuals, and it is fundamental to any serious effort to capture the personality or roles belonging to any individual human being. Thus, players bring their full personalities to an online game, expressing themselves through their avatars and characters. At the same time, game designers create distinctive personalities for the most important non-player characters. *Dark Age of Camelot* has gone so far as to write extensive dialog for its many quest-givers, sometimes requiring the player to communicate with them by typing words into text chat as if they were communicating with a human, in which the non-player characters talk at length about their feelings and past experiences. *Age of Conan* allows the player to ask pre-set personal questions of its quest givers, or to skip this banter, and depending upon the personality of the player, the player may learn much about the personality of the non-player character.

One area of public controversy about online games is the possibility that some people – especially impressionable young people – might become addicted to them. This concern naturally connects to the idea that some personality types might be more vulnerable to addiction. Wang and Chu (2007) have explored this possibility in the light of a recent social-psychological theory that distinguished *harmonious passion* from *obsessive passion*. Vallerand et al. (2003, p. 756) say, "Passion can fuel motivation, enhance well-being, and provide meaning in everyday life. However… passion can also arouse negative emotions, lead to inflexible persistence, and interfere with achieving a balanced, successful life." The former is an harmonious form of passion, while the latter is negative, obsessive, and can amount to addiction. Psychiatrists have long recognized that some people have *obsessive-compulsive* personalities, and in recent years, distinctions have been made between sub-varieties of obsessiveness, for example, in terms of whether or not the individual suffers from an unusual level of anxiety that may fuel compulsive behaviors that serve no positive purpose other than to hold the anxiety in check. However, it is important to distinguish obsessive-compulsive disorder from mere conscientiousness, one of the Big-5 dimensions of normal personality, and, perhaps, the best benchmark is the degree to which the behavior serves the person's general life goals in a manner that is emotionally satisfying without degrading the individual's ability to hold a job and enjoy intimate, real-world social relationships.

Wang and Chu administered a ten-item harmonious-obsessive measurement scale to 404 online game players in Taiwan, using an online questionnaire, as well as a scale measuring Internet addiction. A quarter of these respondents were female; they averaged about eighteen years old, and they typically spent about eighteen hours per week playing online games. Indeed, persons scoring high on addiction tended to score at the obsessive end of the harmonious-obsessive dimension. With studies like this, there is always a question of whether the results indicate a causal connection: obsession causes addiction. An alternate interpretation is that obsession and addiction are overlapping concepts, and some items on each scale to some extent measure the concept of the other scale. But, at the very least, such studies deepen our understanding of the phenomenon and show that it is possible to carry out a range of studies on the personalities of game players, based on diverse concepts.

As Sweetser and Wyeth (2005) correctly argue, it would be a mistake to ignore the ways in which successful games satisfy a wide range of players, quite independently of their personality types. They suggest that the best characteristic a game can have is the capacity to give the player a positive experience of *flow*. This is frankly a rather subjective concept, proposed by a humanistic psychologist, Mihály Csíkszentmihályi, and it has not found favor among rigorous experimentalists in psychology or among cognitive scientists. Yet it is attractive to many members of the general public, and for that very reason may point to key elements of successful, positive human experiences. In the context of computer games, Sweetser and Wyeth say that flow has eight elements:

(1) A task that can be completed;

(2) The ability to concentrate on the task;

(3) That concentration is possible because the task has clear goals;

(4) That concentration is possible because the task provides immediate feedback;

(5) The ability to exercise a sense of control over actions;

(6) A deep but effortless involvement that removes awareness of the frustrations of everyday life;

(7) Concern for self disappears, but sense of self emerges stronger afterwards; and

(8) The sense of the duration of time is altered.

Except for the last two points, it is obvious how advancing toward completion of a quest in a well-designed fantasy game can provide these feelings. I find the seventh point, about the self, rather mystical, but clearly it relates to a feeling of immersion in the game character and some sense of refreshment from playing the game. The final point, an altered sense of the flow of time, is part of the fundamental definition of multiple realities in phenomenology (Schütz, A., 1971), and it ought to be measurable in rigorous studies, so it seems like a reasonable hypothesis to test.

5.4   NON-PLAYER CHARACTER PERSONALITY

The example cited above from *Matrix Online* combines two notions of personality, that of the player with that of the character. Many researchers in and around the field of artificial intelligence have begun exploring how to incorporate principles of real human personality variation in the non-player characters (NPCs) they create. Kshirsagar and Magnenat-Thalmann (2002) used Baysian methods to model NPC mood changes. It is not uncommon for NPCs in existing games to express simulated emotions, such as rage or fear during combat, either roaring and attacking or whimpering and running away. What this study added was the ability to give different NPCs different habitual emotional reactions to events and different common moods, based on three of the five dimensions of the Big-5 theory: "A Neurotic person will change moods often, and tend to go into a negative mood easily. On the other hand, an Extravert person will tend to shift to a positive mood quickly in a conversation. An Agreeable person will tend to go to positive mood more often, but frequent mood changes may not be shown" (Kshirsagar and Magnenat-Thalmann, 2002, p. 110)

Su et al. (2007) also based their research with virtual humans on the Big-5 theory, building a fuzzy rule-based system to combine the influence of different personality characteristics to control the interactions and movements of the virtual character. Starting with the assumption that a character can be high or low on each of the five dimensions, the system produced 32 different rules, such as: If (Openness is Low) and (Conscientiousness is Low) and (Extraversion is Low) and (Agreeableness is Low) and (Neuroticism is Low) then (CharacterType is Hinder) and (BehaviorType is Cold). Arya and Di Paola (2007) developed a system to control facial expressions of virtual humans based on a simpler two-dimensional model: dominance versus submission, and cold versus warm relations with people.

Personality psychology is by no means the only discipline that contributes useful frameworks for understanding players and creating non-player characters. For just one example, there is a well established tradition for understanding emotional meanings in terms of a three-dimensional *semantic differential*. As originally proposed by Osgood et al. (1957), the semantic differential was constructed in a manner rather similar to the Big-5 but focused on the judgments people make of things and events as well as of people. The first dimension is *evaluation*, how good or bad people judge the thing to be. The second dimension is *potency*, and the third is *activity*. A sleeping tiger is low on activity and high on potency; whether it should be evaluated positively depends on whether it is in a cage. Sociologist Heise, D. (2004) has developed a system for giving artificial agents the semantic differential scores of a large number of nouns and verbs, plus a theory about how to combine their meanings into sentences, that potentially would allow the agents to act like human beings in a variety of circumstances.

CHAPTER 6

Avatars and Characters

The player is typically represented in the game environment by one or more characters that have distinctive characteristics such as gender, race, class, profession, mission, and experience level. The relationship between players and their representations inside a gamelike virtual world is a complex one, and it undoubtedly varies by the personality of the player, the nature of the game, and the past history of experiences. Sociologists have long believed that much can be learned about human beings from studying the roles and games they play (Pangburn, W., 1922; Stanton et al., 1956).

6.1   BUILDING A BOND WITH AN AVATAR

Let me tell you about my two main *World of Warcraft* characters, Maxrohn the level 75 Human priest and Catullus the level 80 Blood Elf priest. Just now, I logged into each in turn and entered "/played" into the text chat. The system then told me the total time I had run each of them over the past two and a half years: Maxrohn = 33 days, 9 hours, 52 minutes, 46 seconds; Catullus = 32 days, 15 hours, 35 minutes, 38 seconds. Given that those are 24-hour days, I have invested nearly 800 hours in each of them. This is more time than I estimate I have invested in any of my co-workers at my real-world job, which I have held for seventeen years, if only because employment relationships in real-world jobs these days tend to be fragmentary and fleeting. The point is that many game players invest so much time in their characters, often "sharing" intensely emotional experiences with them, that they can become extremely meaningful.

We also invest meaning in characters when we create and develop them. Maxrohn was my first priest, and I named him after my uncle, Max Rohn, who was an Episcopal priest but had died some years before. Max was something of an adventurer as well as a cleric, who held churches on remote islands in the sea and once taught me a judo move that could break a man's arm. Maxrohn developed a rich personality over my 800 hours working with him, that was a mixture of my own personality and what I recalled about my uncle. Not many players may name their characters after colorful, deceased relatives, but all probably invest in their characters some of their prior feelings about real people they have known in their lives.

It is also true that highly-developed characters develop a will of their own. As radical as this idea may seem, I suggest it is literally true, given how the human mind functions. As the extreme cases of multiple-personality neurosis and veteran movie actors illustrate, a human being can adopt multiple roles that operate like semi-autonomous personalities. This is how we are able to interact with other people, by forming in our own minds models of the other person's thought processes and desires. In the case of Catullus, I originally thought of him as a reflection of the ancient Roman poet, Catullus, perhaps, with a little of Julius Caesar thrown in, and even some elements of my two Latin teachers. Like the ancient Romans, Blood Elves are arrogant, technically competent, hedonistic, and cynical. Those are my character's characteristics. My Catullus (2008) has actually published a book chapter under his own name, in which he debates his own existence and his right to become autonomous from my control. How real is that?

To consider a game character to be somewhat real, we need to grant reality to the world he lives in. Based on consideration of narrative theory and a range of previous scholarship, Ryan, M. (2001) has suggested that a player's relationship to an electronic game can be described in terms of two largely independent dimensions: Internal-External and Ontological-Exploratory. The Internal-External dimension concerns how much the individual becomes immersed inside the game world, whether by identifying closely with an avatar or because the computer technology produces a highly realistic world the user experiences from a first person perspective. The Ontological-Exploratory dimension concerns how much the user can affect what happens in the virtual environment, very much at the Ontological extreme of the dimension, versus hardly at all at the Exploratory extreme. Thus, the most realistic situation combines Internal with Ontological, but the two dimensions are conceptually separate, and Ryan shows there are examples of the four logical categories created by crosscutting these two dichotomies.

Users differ greatly in terms of their orientation toward immersion and how they conceptualize their digital representations. The naive view of many observers and some players holds that the digital image that hops when the user presses the space bar directly represents the user. This view is implied by the term *avatar*, which originally meant the terrestrial reflection of a Hindu deity. The avatar is simpler than the deity or user, perhaps, representing just some aspects, but it does possess the identity of the deity or user to a significant degree. Non-game virtual worlds like *Second Life* tend to use the term *avatar*, but online games do not, preferring the term *character*. One reason is that successful games encourage users to have multiple characters, with different capabilities and perhaps different personalities to match, thereby giving the user a more varied experience and keeping the user in the game longer. This suggests a third possible dimension crosscutting the two defined by Ryan, perhaps called Unitary-Multiple. All these are matters of degree, and the Unitary situation is comparable to reading a novel, whereas the Multiple situation is like reading a collection of short stories about different characters.

A few gamelike virtual worlds do not represent the player by a humanoid avatar, notably *Jumpgate* and *EVE Online*, which use spaceships instead. Figure 6.1 shows the very complex display in *EVE Online*, just as I am being defeated and my ship is about to explode. In theory, the ship is piloted by a character named Theo who is a priest of the Amarr Empire, and a thumbnail picture of him is in the upper left corner of the screenshot. But the primary experience of *EVE* is piloting the ship myself. The navigation aids in this game are excellent, such as the list of nearby targets at the right of the picture, but take many hours to learn. We do not need an avatar when we drive a car in the real world, so why do we need one to drive a spaceship in a virtual world?

First-person shooters differ in terms of the degree to which they assign a specific fictional identity to the first-person character, or they let the users feel they are operating their gun directly. Much of the time I spend in *Second Life* is creating virtual objects and putting programs into them,

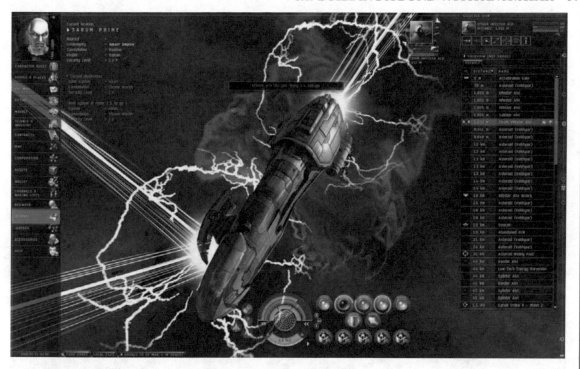

Figure 6.1: Being Defeated in *EVE Online*.

during which time my avatar is an annoying hindrance. So, for all the legitimate research interest in player-avatar relations, we must keep in mind that there are at least two other alternatives: characters not conceptualized as representing the player, and working directly through an impersonal user, interface with neither a character nor an avatar.

The games themselves need not be constrained by these categories, and they sometimes combine them as in *Pirates of the Burning Sea*. Figure 6.2 shows my first ship in combat with a pirate who will shortly be sunk by my cannon. My ship is in the center, and if I zoom the viewpoint inward, I can see my men working on its deck. Usually, it is more effective to zoom back and see more of the surrounding sea, watching the ship condition display in the upper left corner, and having no consciousness of any avatar but the vessel. However, I often have the choice to board the other ship, at which point I see the battle from the standpoint of my avatar, Edmund Bainbridge, brandishing his cutlass. *Pirates of the Burning Sea* is a fairly realistic depiction of commerce and navel competition in 1720, and I selected for my avatar an actual ancestor of mine who was 18 years old in that year and had the correct personality to be a freetrader. Depending on the mission, my experience switches between a focus on the avatar or a focus on the vessel. Given the word's multiple meanings, *vessel* would be a good generic term to use whenever a player is represented by something other than an in-game person.

Figure 6.2: A Sea Battle in *Pirates of the Burning Sea*.

6.2 THE QUALITY OF AVATAR RELATIONSHIPS

A number of researchers are exploring the extent to which avatars and game characters express a person's ideal self, are similar to the individual's own personality, or possess identities of their own (Schultze and Leahy, 2009). People have a variety of relationships with their game characters, and Blinka, L. (2008) did a questionnaire study of *EverQuest* and *World of Warcraft* players to determine whether the level of maturity of the player shaped this variation. A factor analysis distinguished three dimensions of the relationships. *Identification* is the degree to which the player feels similar to the character, and *compensation* is the degree to which the player would wish to be more like the character. The strength of identification was greater among young and presumably immature players, but the data did not permit fully testing age differences with compensation. *Immersion* is the extent to which the player feels emotionally involved with the character, for example, feeling ashamed or proud of what the character does and thinking about the character even while not playing. This factor does not correlate with age, but it may be stronger among men and among unmarried people.

Blinka noted that only 4 percent of women play a male character, but 23 percent of men play a female character.

Playing these games extensively conceivably could produce maturity in the sense discovered by Blinka because advanced players often have multiple characters, and thus they develop a range of kinds of relationships to them. My own example, having run about three dozen characters for at least a work week each, may be extreme, but the whole point of games offering a variety of characters is to encourage subscribers to stay longer by exploring many of them.

In a questionnaire study of *World of Warcraft* players, Bessiere et al. (2007) had people rate themselves, their ideal self, and their main character along a number of psychological scales. They found that the character was more like the ideal self along three of the Big-5 personality dimensions: conscientiousness, extraversion, and neuroticism. This tended to be especially the case for people who felt depressed and had low self-esteem. The question then arises whether playing a successful character could possibly reduce depression and raise self-esteem of the player, even outside the game situation. Current research cannot answer this question, but we can imagine longitudinal studies to explore it rigorously. For present purposes, the point is that player-character relations may change over time for any given player or category of players, as well as differing from one player to another.

To compare avatar-creation systems and explore physical appearance dimensions of the player-character relationship, Ducheneaut et al. (2009) administered questionnaires to people who use three very different virtual worlds (VWs), *World of Warcraft*, *Maplestory*, which is a two-dimensional multiplayer role-playing game, and the non-game virtual world, *Second Life*. Males were more likely to create an avatar of the opposite gender than females were, and older people tended to make their avatars appear younger. Players in all three environments considered the style and color of their character's hair to be a high-impact decision, and overweight players tend to prefer slimmer characters. This study also asked respondents to rate both themselves and their main characters on the Big-5 personality dimensions, finding they rated their characters more conscientious and extraverted but less neurotic than they considered themselves to be. However, the novel findings of this study concern physical appearance:

> Our data also show that VWs are used to experiment with digital bodies that are often very different from a user's. In a large majority of cases, VWs users create a digital identity that looks close to Western ideals: leaner, younger, more fashionable versions of themselves. This trend is particularly prevalent for older users and those with weight issues, but it also benefits these users more – they are more satisfied and more attached to their enhanced online selves than average. While such "perfect bodies" therefore appear to have clear benefits to some, it is also worth mentioning that it may cause VWs to become much less diverse than physical environments in the long run, which may in turn lead users to a fairly stereotyped vision of what a human body should be (Ducheneaut et al., 2009, p. 1160).

Huh and Williams (2010) have looked closely at gender-switching in *EverQuest 2*, employing a rich dataset combining a questionnaire administered to a large number of players with information directly about their characters from the game servers. The most striking finding was that few players switch genders when creating a character, and, apparently, free exploration of a new identity is not a major factor motivating people to play these games. A set of suggestive findings chiefly concerning female players indicated that this general rule did not apply to everybody. One category of female players did appear to be ambivalent about their conventionally defined gender, adopted male characters, and behaved in what might be described as a hyper-masculine fashion.

Fron et al. (2007) note that scholars have tended to dismiss the tendency of humans to explore different ways of appearing by trying on various kinds of clothing and dressing up for public display: "From a feminist perspective, we can look at dress-up, which has historically been associated with female play, as fulcrum for the creation of more gender-inclusive games, as well as a bridge to more gender-balanced approaches to game studies."

Barr et al. (2006) have noted that avatars frequently change their appearance, behavioral abilities, and other characteristics during solo-player computer games, and this is certainly true for the longer-duration online role-playing games. Both *World of Warcraft* and *Entropia Universe* allow characters to get haircuts. Quests in many games put the character in disguise. For example, several quests in both *Dark Age of Camelot* and *World of Warcraft* involve donning a disguise to get into an enemy camp to overhear their secret plans.

More research will be needed to determine the range of meanings people attach to gender swapping and other situations in which players create game characters that are very different from themselves (Hussain and Griffiths, 2008). However, I must suggest that the answer to such questions may not be stable, either across games or across the passing years. For example, when people first started interacting online, many observers feared this reflected or could cause social isolation, yet those concerns largely evaporated as online communications matured. It may be that a significant fraction of people attracted to online games today have unusual motivations, and that as this new medium grows, its users will become more like the general public.

It is also true that each player gains experience that may radically change relationships with characters. In my own case, I must admit some trepidation when I created my first female character, a hesitation that had vanished by the time I had created my tenth. From my own perspective, they are characters with some degree of individual integrity of their own, just like the characters of many types created by a novelist, and I don't think of them as avatars any of which represent my self-image or my ideal. Different people will approach these issues in a wide variety of ways that are likely to shift as the industry matures, giving researchers many years of interesting work to understand this historic evolution.

6.3 SECONDARY AVATARS

As we have noted, experienced players of these games tend to operate multiple characters. If a player concentrates on one character to the exclusions of others, then it is the player's *main*, and the others are *alts*. But we have also referred to secondary avatars, and there has been very little research to my knowledge about these avatars of avatars. The games conceptualize them in various different ways, for example, a coder character in *Matrix Online*, who has acquired the right programming skills can create a *proxy*, to help fight or even to heal the main avatar. The user interface panel for controlling a proxy has displays for health and inner strength, just like the main character, plus two sets of buttons with which to give commands. Three buttons at the left set the temperament of the assistant: aggressive, passive, or fighting enemies only when they attack. A set of four buttons on the right tell the assistant whether to attack the selected target, follow the main avatar, stay in its present location, or cease to exist. On occasion I had told a proxy to stay where he was, then I walked as far as a virtual city block away and called him to come. Surprisingly, even when the route was complex, he often found his way.

Perhaps the archetype of secondary avatars is a hunter's pet in *World of Warcraft*. First, a hunter must tame a wild animal, give it a name, and begin to train it. At even a fairly low level of experience, the pet's control bar includes common commands like attack, follow, and stay – or moods like aggressive, passive, or defensive. Also the pet may be made to growl at the enemy to get it to focus on the pet rather than the main character, prowl in stealth mode so the enemy won't notice it, and claw or rake at the enemy. Other user interface options feed or heal the pet, and the player even can look though the eyes of the pet when it goes scouting.

While games differ, something like a convention has emerged about the primary controls used to operate a secondary avatar. Here are primary modes and commands *Lord of the Rings Online* offers for bear pets, plus a couple of the more complex options:

Aggressive Mode - Your pet will enter combat when valid targets are detected.

Passive Mode - Your pet will not enter combat unless commanded to.

Guard Mode - Your pet will enter combat to defend you or itself.

Attack - Your pet will attack your currently selected target.

Follow - Your pet will move towards you and then act according to its mode.

Stay - Your pet will stay in its current position unless its mode requires combat.

Toggle Assist - When enabled, your pet will attack targets that you attack.

Roaring Challenge - This skill forces the target to attack the bear.

Sign of the Wild: Rage - This sign asks your animal friend to go into a rage, attacking faster and making itself look as threatening as possible.

Extreme examples of specialized secondary avatars can be found in *Age of Conan*, where necromancer characters can command entire teams. Figure 6.3 shows Eridanos and his team of six, just as they retrieve a relic from Atlantis called the Phoenix of the North in a heavily defended ice cave in the Eiglophina Mountains, after killing a witch named Mithrelle. In the center, proudly dressed in his white robe, is Eridanos the level 52 Stygian necromancer. Immediately behind him are two deathless acolytes, an arcanist and a mage, who supplement his damaging spells. The other four assistants are undead minions. At the far left are a life-stealer that takes life from the enemy and gives it to the team, and a mutilator that inflicts bleeding wounds. On the right side of the picture are a corruptor that adds additional holy damage to each attack and a harvester that gives the team mana and stamina.

Figure 6.3: Eridanos with Secondary Avatars in *Age of Conan*.

Games differ in terms of how much they personalize secondary avatars. In *World of Warcraft*, for example, the player names a hunter's pet, and when it dies, it is revived with the same identity, whereas a Warlock's minion is summoned from another realm and cannot be given a distinctive name. The proxies in *Matrix Online* appear at random male or female each time one is summoned, dressed like local gang members with unpredictable weapons specialization, and cannot be named. In order to name the robot Tobor in *Anarchy Online*, I needed to write a simple macro program and run it whenever I generated a robot, so that game allowed me to personalize the secondary avatar but did not require it. In the much more recent game, *Lord of the Rings Online*, Rumilisoun easily gave her sturdy bear the permanent name Beorn, her aloof raven the name Poe, and her stealthy lynx the name Lamhainn. Given their complexity and their potential to be meaningful to players, secondary avatars would be a fruitful topic for future research.

6.4   FACING THE END

Perhaps the most profound question for player-character relations is death. Lisbeth Klastrup has written repeatedly about this, and she notes that death in the games always allows the possibility of resurrection, whereas death for players is *permadeath*, from which there is no obvious worldly salvation. Klastrup, L. (2006) suggests that in this context death has four possible meanings:

- Avatar death as in-game mechanics (concrete death).

- Death as a symbolic event visualized in a variety of forms.

- Avatar death as narrativised event in the life of an avatar.

- The death of a player.

In another essay, Klastrup, L. (2008) describes the in-game mechanics of death in *World of Warcraft*. First, the player sees the character fall on the ground, then a dialog box opens asking if the player wants the character to resurrect at the nearest graveyard. If no other player casts a resurrection spell, the character teleports to the graveyard in six minutes, even without a click in the box. The character is not immediately restored to life at the graveyard but exists in a shadowy state, in which the world appears colorless, until either the player decides to accept the offer of resurrection from an angel, which leaves the character temporarily weakened, or the character runs back to its corpse and resurrects itself.

Games differ in how death is handled, and some do not even permit a player's character to die. In *Lord of the Rings Online*, the character merely retreats in a weakened condition. In *EVE Online*, the character escapes from his or her spaceship in a pod, which seems gentle enough except that the loss of a spaceship is extremely costly. In *Dark Age of Camelot*, so the mythos says, magical stones fell from heaven after the death of King Arthur, and deceased avatars revive at whichever of these stones they most recently bound themselves to, which can be very far away from where they died, rather than nearby as in *World of Warcraft*. The character must pay a healer to restore lost strength to them, and they can return to the scenes of their deaths to regain some lost experience. This is done, dramatically enough, by kneeling in prayer at their own tombstones.

Klastrup' second meaning of death, as a symbolic event, suggests that the death and resurrection of a player's character may have emotional, philosophical, or even religious meaning for the player. Two of my own favorite avatars, Cosmic Engineer and William Bridgebain, died permanently when *Matrix Online* and *Tabula Rasa* were closed down. A total of thirty others died, nearly permanently, when I cancelled my subscriptions after completing the intended research, although many game companies keep the characters on file in cases the player wants to reactivate the account. Yes, it is sad to lose an old friend, although players undoubtedly differ in the degree to which they conceptualize the termination of their characters in this way.

Klastrup' third meaning recognizes that the life of an avatar is a story, and death can conclude a chapter of that narrative, as when a brave comrade sacrifices life for his or her guildmates in an heroic battle. The fourth meaning, permadeath of a player, raises the challenging question of whether characters could live on after their players' deaths, perhaps, operated by some form of artificial intelligence that had used machine learning to archive the players style. Readers who dismiss this idea as foolish and superficial should meditate upon the fact that they can interact with a deceased person's avatar on the Aldor Rise in Shattrath City, in *World of Warcraft*. At age 28, a player named Dak Krause died of leukemia, and his level 70 Night Elf huntress, Caylee Dak, was placed in the game as a memorial. Her one function in the game is to receive a sentimental poem about death sent to her from a little girl character, and to bless the person who delivers it.

CHAPTER 7

Virtual Professions and Economies

Long-duration games often invest a good deal of the action into the production and sales of virtual goods by players, using elaborate systems of resource gathering, item crafting, and exchange through complex auction houses. One of the ways to win status is to excel in one or more professions. For example, in *Entropia Universe*, the public text chat abounds with messages like these:

- Max aka Cayenne found a deposit (Lytairian Dust) with a value of 72 PED!

- Aleksandra Mayday Kowalski found a deposit (Copper Stone) with a value of 99 PED!

- Ericsson Cozzmo Kramer killed a creature (Atrox Young) with a value of 135 PED!

- Team "Jedi & Trooper" killed a creature (Hogglo Young) with a value of 61 PED!

- Tom Psychodadiks Delonge killed a creature (Aurli Watcher) with a value of 286 PED and has been recorded in the Hall of Fame!

- Anunka Mithra Skarpnes manufactured an item (Zombie Arm Guards (M,L)) worth 829 PED and has been recorded in the Hall of Fame!

"PED" in these messages refers to Project Entropia Dollars, ten of which nominally equal a US dollar, so that 829 PED equals $82.90. Thus, people are winning money as well as fame, and depending upon your perspective, that sounds either like a game or like capitalism. In some games, practicing a profession can be an alternate way of advancing in the main status contest, comparable to completing quests and killing enemies, depending on the specialization of the character. An engineer in *Star Wars Galaxies* does not get any status advantage from killing an enemy, but he does from collecting materials from the environment and assembling them to create a robot, whereas a Jedi knight chiefly gains status by slaughtering enemies with a light saber. More commonly, however, online games have separate systems of honor and advancement for ordinary adventuring versus specialized professions, permitting any character to do both in whatever mixture the player desires, although access to economic resources depends heavily upon advancement in combat experience.

7.1 WORK IN *STAR WARS GALAXIES*

To compare the extremes in careers of MMORPG characters, I ran two some distance up the status ladder in *Star Wars Galaxies*, an engineer named Algorithma Teq and a Jedi named Simula

Tion. While Simula was gallivanting around doing heroic quests for characters like Jabba the Hut, Algorithma was plodding around the planet Tatooine laboriously collecting raw materials and using a series of tools to craft them into valuable virtual devices, including the tools themselves.

Many games allow characters to gather various resources from the natural environment, but they differ in the restrictions they place on which characters can gather which resources, what virtual tools are required to gain a resource, and what information is provided to the player about the resources that exist in the vicinity. In *Entropia Universe*, any player can acquire and develop proficiency with prospecting tools, but there are no hints about what resources might be nearby before the tool sets off a little explosion or sends a probe down a hole, and doing so uses up one of the explosives or probes the player has earlier purchased. In *Tale in the Desert*, a character looking for slate to make blades knows to walk along a shoreline until a slate icon appears at the top of the screen and to click on the icon to tell the character to bend down and pick up the stone. A miner or herbalist in *World of Warcraft* can set the little map in the interface to display a gold dot indicating resources but only nearby and only for characters trained in the appropriate profession.

When Algorithma went prospecting, she had to have the right tool and decide when to use it, although doing so was costly only in terms of time. She had to tell the tool exactly which resource to search for, and Figure 7.1 shows the display after she has found some Didoreo, which is a variety of Agrinium, which is a variety of Aluminum, which is in the non-ferrous metal category. On the left, the display shows a map of the vicinity, with percentages indicating the chance of getting Didoreo at each location. When she started, at some distance from her final location, the percentages were very low, even 0%, but in one direction, they were slightly higher, so she walked that way. Again and again, she would prospect, see which direction had the higher percentages, and go in that direction, until she found a good place to stop and extract the needed Didoreo. Eventually, even a rich deposit becomes depleted, and she would need to resume prospecting.

Many games require a character to have both skills and instructions, as well as raw materials, before being able to create a particular virtual object or substance. Depending upon the game, skills are acquired through training, which may cost money, or through experience doing similar but easier work in the past. Instructions take the form of a recipe or schematic, which may be found in the field, bought from a vendor, traded between players, or automatically acquired at some level of general experience.

Early in her development, Algorithma made a chemical survey device, which she could then use in her own prospecting. Figure 7.2 shows what her display looked like at step two out of six. The display explains, "This tool scans the local environment for chemical resources than can be extracted with the appropriate types of harvesters and even has the ability to acquire minute samples of the resources it detects." This implies that an advanced engineer will need a whole toolkit of specialized devices, each of which may be manufactured in this manner. To make this device, she needs a generic crafting tool, which she can also use to make more advanced or specialized crafting tools able to do more advanced projects. She also needs the schematic, which has "instructions" (she cannot read them, but they permit the required manufacturing steps) on how to make and assemble

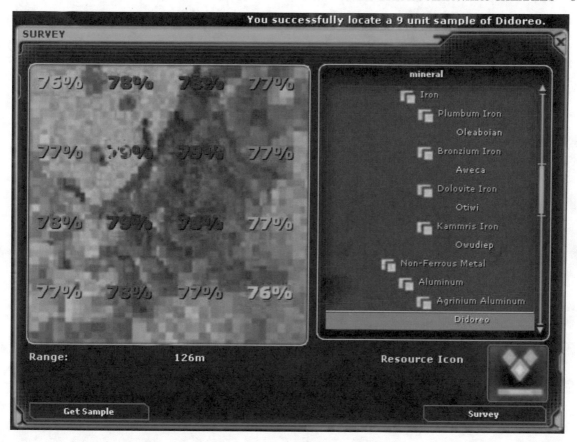

Figure 7.1: Prospecting for Resources in *Star Wars Galaxies*.

four subcomponents, in this case: the assembly enclosure, the controller mechanism, the scanner assembly, and the storage unit. On the left side of the display are the relevant resources she already possesses, and she has most recently selected amorphous gemstone, which she earlier intentionally prospected for and collected. At this point, she is ready to assemble the subcomponents, which she will do by clicking the [Assemble] button at the lower right.

Although this is an extreme example, very commonly games represent creation of economic value in terms of gathering raw materials, gaining technical abilities, and going through a complex series of steps to achieve the desired goal. This is a nice metaphor for how any real economy works, aside from the market mechanisms that handle investment and exchange. But it is also a model of how computer programming works, based on *algorithms* which are precise sets of instructions for achieving a given goal in a finite number of steps.

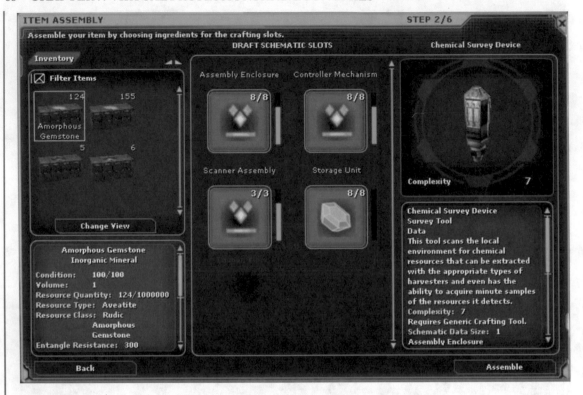

Figure 7.2: Making a Simple Device in *Star Wars Galaxies*.

A final point about the division of labor in *Star Wars Galaxies* is valuable both in understanding how gameworlds evolve and in recognizing the care that researchers must exercise when relying upon publications. In November 2005, a major update called the New Game Enhancements radically transformed the way the different professions and character lines worked, including letting players start a character as a Jedi and greatly simplifying the development lines for the existing professions such as engineers. Prior to this transformation, a guidebook had been published, *Star Wars Galaxies: The Total Experience* (McCubbin et al., 2005), which describes the situation prior to this change in great detail, so a researcher or student must not assume it describes the game as it existed after this revolution. Reportedly, many players who were heavily invested in the earlier system left the game in disgust, but players who joined later may have found the new system more comfortable.

7.2   PRODUCTION IN *WORLD OF WARCRAFT*

The most successful internal economy of any multiplayer game is the one in *World of Warcraft* at the very least because so many players engage in it, rendering the marketplace rich with the virtual resources they gather and exchange. To illustrate how statistical analysis can be performed in studies of games, I will use two quantitative datasets I collected at some effort. One dataset covers professions and several other variables about 1,096 members of the Alea Iacta Est guild on the Earthen Ring server, all those who were level 10 or above in the period February 17-22, 2008, a guild that will be described more fully later. To draw a sample for the other dataset, I used the CensusPlus add-on program to identify of all characters online at any point during Saturday, January 12, 2008, on two contrasting other servers, Emerald Dream and Scarlet Crusade. The former is a PvP server, while the latter is not, so to get a balanced sample, I removed 97 cases at random from Emerald Dream. The actual data in both cases came from manually looking up each of these characters in *World of Warcraft's* online database, The Armory[1].

A character in *World of Warcraft* can perform any of the three secondary professions – fishing, cooking, and first aid – but only two of the ten primary professions that were available for most of the 2007-2008 period: alchemy, blacksmithing, enchanting, engineering, herbalism, jewelcrafting, leatherworking, mining, skinning, and tailoring. Developing skill in any of these takes a considerable investment of time and effort, so while characters may switch professions, they tend to be locked into the ones they learned when they were around level 10 in general experience.

At a first approximation, there are two categories of professions, *gathering* and *crafting*. Gathering professions collect resources from the landscape. Miners collect ore from which metals and gems can be extracted; herbalists collect plants that serve as ingredients for potions, and skinners take leather from the corpses of animals. These resources can be traded directly to other players, placed on the auction house, or sold to non-player characters called *vendors*. Thus, they are economic resources. In harvesting these resources, characters compete with each other, but skinning also has an implicit cooperative aspect. Often, a skinner comes across the corpses of dead animals killed by non-skinners and can take their hides without the inconvenience of killing them first. A gatherer gains skill mainly by gathering, with rare trips to a non-player trainer, and increasing skill is required to gather increasingly valuable resources.

Crafting professions involve manufacturing useful goods from raw materials, so they have a dual relationship to the division of labor and economic exchange. First, the crafter must obtain the necessary raw materials, either by gathering them personally or by purchasing them. For example, an engineer can make a nice, functioning telescope called the "ornate spyglass," by assembling 2 bronze tubes, 2 whirring bronze gizmos, 1 copper modulator, and one 1 moss agate gem. Each tube, in turn, requires 2 bronze bars and 1 weak flux; each gizmo requires 2 bronze bars and 1 wool cloth; each modulator requires 1 copper bar, 2 linen cloths, and 2 handfuls of copper bolts. A handful of bolts, in turn, requires 1 copper bar. The moss agate gem is somewhat rare, so engineers tend to buy it on the auction house even if they have the mining profession and use it to get the copper plus the tin that makes bronze when alloyed with copper.

Second, the crafter sells at least some of the goods produced, in order to have the money needed to buy materials. In addition, but not involving other players, crafters must purchase frequent training

---

[1]http://www.wowarmory.com/

from non-player trainers to gain the skills required to make particular goods, in an ascending ladder of abilities. One profession, enchanting, has aspects of gathering as well as crafting because enchanters can obtain some of the materials they need by disenchanting already-enchanted objects they loot from non-player enemies.

There are two ways of evaluating the utility of a profession: in terms of its value for the individual player, or for its value to other players in the individual's guild. Among the most obvious kinds of utility for the individual are whether the profession can craft the armor that the given player can wear. Mages, priests, and warlocks can use only cloth armor, which can be crafted by tailors. Below level 40, druids, hunters, rogues and shamans can use only leather armor, made by leatherworkers. Paladins and warriors use metal armor, made by blacksmiths. Thus, one important variable is whether or not characters can make their own armor.

All characters loot the cloth required by tailors, but leatherworkers rely upon skinners to provide their raw materials, and blacksmiths similarly rely upon miners for the smelted metals they require. Therefore, it is worth asking whether leatherworkers and blacksmiths have the second profession required for their own craft. Those who wear cloth armor, naturally are least well protected, so they may benefit from the craft of enchanting more than other classes. Furthermore, enchanters can craft magic wands, which are used by the same three classes that wear cloth, so enchanting and tailoring are linked indirectly, as well.

Table 7.1 shows the percentages for each class practicing each profession where the numbers are at least 20 percent, across the two data samples. Printed in bold are the professions that produce the given class's armor – such as blacksmithing for warriors – plus the profession that supports the particular kind of armor-making. We can see that mining is popular across most classes, and this is the case because the metal and gems obtained through mining are needed by fully three of the crafting professions: blacksmithing, engineering, and jewelcrafting.

7.3   DIVISION OF LABOR IN PROFESSIONS

The professions practiced by characters in many online games represent a sophisticated system of division of labor (Durkheim, E., 1933), and they possess complex economic interconnections. We shall first look at connections between major professions in *World of Warcraft*, then briefly compare with three other examples.

Table 7.1 shows that each *World of Warcraft* class rates highly the gathering profession that provides the raw material for its own kind of armor. Characters creating their own armor and gathering the raw material for it themselves are more self-reliant and, therefore, less dependent upon their group, than other characters, all else being equal. On the other hand, some characters practice two of the three pure raw-material professions (skinning, mining, and herbalism), often with the aim of selling the materials to non-player vendors or on an auction house. Other pairs of professions also have practical links, so it is worth analyzing the connections between professions.

Table 7.2 shows how popular each profession is, plus its statistical connection with other professions. The correlations are the Pearson r coefficient, which ranges from -1.00 through zero

Table 7.1: Professions Preferred by *World of Warcraft* Classes.

Class	Alea Iacta Est (1,096)	Two Realms (1,420)
Warrior	**Mining 71%**	**Mining 73%**
	Blacksmithing 37%	**Blacksmithing 53%**
	Herbalism 28%	
Paladin	**Mining 80%**	**Mining 71%**
	Blacksmithing 34%	**Blacksmithing 40%**
Rogue	**Skinning 50%**	**Skinning 43%**
	Mining 36%	**Leatherworking 37%**
	Leatherworking 32%	Mining 31%
	Engineering 22%	Engineering 23%
		Herbalism 21%
Hunter	**Skinning 59%**	**Skinning 51%**
	Mining 43%	Mining 41%
	Leatherworking 33%	**Leatherworking 36%**
		Engineering 21%
Druid	**Skinning 63%**	Herbalism 43%
	Herbalism 42%	**Skinning 40%**
	Leatherworking 31%	Alchemy 32%
	Alchemy 20%	**Leatherworking 24%**
Shaman	**Skinning 41%**	Mining 43%
	Herbalism 38%	**Skinning 30%**
	Mining 32%	Jewelcrafting 24%
	Alchemy 26%	**Leatherworking 24%**
	Leatherworking 20%	Herbalism 23%
Warlock	**Tailoring 53%**	**Tailoring 48%**
	Enchanting 38%	**Enchanting 39%**
	Mining 29%	Mining 31%
	Skinning 24%	
Mage	**Tailoring 46%**	**Tailoring 44%**
	Enchanting 46%	**Enchanting 41%**
	Mining 29%	Mining 30%
	Herbalism 22%	
Priest	**Tailoring 54%**	**Tailoring 53%**
	Enchanting 41%	**Enchanting 36%**
	Herbalism 27%	Mining 27%
	Mining 25%	Herbalism 20%
	Skinning 21%	

Table 7.2: Correlations between Professions in *World of Warcraft*.

	Alea Iacta Est (1,096)		Two Realms (1,420)	
Profession	Percent	Correlations	Percent	Correlations
Alchemy	14.3%	**Herbalism 0.66** *Tailoring –0.28* *Skinning –0.31* *Mining –0.33*	14.7%	**Herbalism 0.78** *Skinning –0.25* *Mining –0.33*
Blacksmithing	7.6%	**Mining 0.31** *Skinning –0.21* *Tailoring –0.24*	12.1%	**Mining 0.37** *Skinning –0.21*
Enchanting	19.6%	**Tailoring 0.54** *Herbalism –0.21* *Leatherworking –0.21* *Mining –0.26* *Skinning –0.28*	19.8%	**Tailoring 0.48** *Herbalism –0.20* *Leatherworking –0.20* *Skinning –0.20* *Mining –0.26*
Engineering	10.3%	**Mining 0.29** *Skinning –0.25*	13.2%	**Mining 0.30** *Skinning –0.21*
Herbalism	23.4%	**Alchemy 0.66** *Enchanting –0.21* *Tailoring –0.22* *Leatherworking –0.23* *Mining –0.33*	19.3%	**Alchemy 0.78** *Enchanting –0.20* *Leatherworking –0.21* *Mining –0.32*
Jewelcrafting	6.4%	**Mining 0.24** *Skinning –0.20*	9.9%	**Mining 0.24**
Leatherworking	15.0%	**Skinning 0.55** *Tailoring –0.20* *Enchanting –0.21* *Herbalism –0.23* *Mining –0.34*	15.7%	**Skinning 0.66** *Enchanting –0.20* *Herbalism –0.21* *Mining –0.35*
Mining	40.6%	**Blacksmithing 0.31** **Engineering 0.29** **Jewelcrafting 0.24** *Enchanting –0.26* *Tailoring –0.28* *Alchemy –0.33* *Herbalism –0.33* *Leatherworking –0.34*	40.4%	**Blacksmithing 0.37** **Engineering 0.30** **Jewelcrafting 0.24** *Enchanting –0.26* *Skinning –0.26* *Tailoring –0.30* *Herbalism –0.32* *Alchemy –0.33* *Leatherworking –0.35*
Skinning	36.3%	**Leatherworking 0.55** *Blacksmithing –0.21* *Engineering –0.25* *Tailoring –0.28* *Enchanting –0.28* *Alchemy –0.31*	26.9%	**Leatherworking 0.66** *Enchanting –0.20* *Blacksmithing –0.21* *Engineering –0.21* *Alchemy –0.25* *Mining –0.26*
Tailoring	18.7%	**Enchanting 0.54** *Leatherworking –0.20* *Herbalism –0.22* *Skinning –0.24* *Alchemy –0.28*	16.6%	**Enchanting 0.48** *Alchemy –0.30*

to +1.00, and measures the negative or positive associations between pairs of variables. There is a built-in negative correlation because selecting one profession uses up one of the two choices and thus makes it less likely to select any other profession. All coefficients shown are statistically significant, and the table focuses just on those with a respectable magnitude, at least 0.20 from zero in either direction. The very strong connections between alchemy and herbalism (0.66, 0.78) reflect the fact that herbs are among the raw materials needed by alchemists to make their magic potions.

Less than half of the characters could make the armor they themselves wore. This implies they often relied upon other players to create their armor for them, and they produced other goods to provide in turn. It implies that the entire system is set up in such as way as to encourage cooperation between players in industry as well as battle. However, one of the motivations for having multiple characters is to practice multiple trade skills, and the multiple characters belonging to one player can send goods and virtual money to each other through the in-game mail system. Note that both possibilities encourage players to keep paying their subscriptions. Economic exchange with other players builds social bonds that become valuable in themselves and thus a source of commitment (Homans, G., 1950). Developing multiple characters increases the time a player must play.

Compared with *World of Warcraft*, *Dark Age of Camelot* does not have a complete, modern economic system of resource extraction, production and exchange. There are six trade skills: alchemy, armorcraft, fletching (arrow-making), spellcraft, tailoring, and weaponcrafting. Production is not a full economic system. Characters can learn only certain crafting skills, depending on the class to which they belong, and they cannot make anything they themselves cannot use. Raw materials must be bought from non-player characters, rather than gathered from the environment. There is no elaborate auction system, such as in *World of Warcraft* and other more recent games, and trading takes place between individual players. In the case of spellcrafting and alchemy, this makes perfect sense because the crafter often enhances an item the customer already possesses. But the primitive nature of exchange also fits a Dark Ages society where the economy is largely based on barter.

The Matrix Online allowed any character to practice any number of skills, although gaining them all was a tremendous labor and players tended to specialize. When near one of the hardline telephone booths that functioned as an interface to the fictional mainframe computers, a player could switch various program modules in and out of inventory, gaining access to the corresponding skills, limited only by the number that could be carried at once by a character at the given experience level, and by the fact the player needed to have earned the skill and placed it in inventory. Thus, players who wanted to experience different specializations, whether of crafting or combat, did not need to have multiple characters, a fact that compensated to some extent for how tedious leveling up tended to be at the higher levels.

Because it lacks quests and similar lore-based adventures, *Entropia Universe* relies more heavily than the other examples on gathering resources and crafting virtual items. Prospecting for mineral resources requires explosive charges and probes that are destroyed in the process of using them, and they need to be bought from vending machines where weapon ammunition, animal decoys, and other perishable items need to be bought as well. This was a key part of the larger economic system, because the money to buy these commodities comes from exchanging external currencies like US dollars for the internal currency, Project Entropia Dollars.

Crafting must be done at machines found in cities or outposts, but this is not an inconvenience, because at the same location can be found the character's storage locker and an auctioneer from which materials can be bought. Once an item had been made, it can be sold to a vending machine for a set price, which was usually done when the player was crafting for the purpose of building up the character's skill level and thus making things that no other player might want, but it also can be sold to another player through the auctioneer. Despite the fact that the auction system in *Entropia Universe* tends to have far fewer items for sale than the *World of Warcraft* system, it works well, because many of the items for sale indeed find customers, and patient players can check the system frequently to see what had just been put up for sale and either buy it outright for a high price or place a bid just above the previous high bid. Given the great effort required to gain a high skill level, players tend to specialize, and there is no economic advantage in having multiple characters.

CHAPTER 8

Social Relations Inside Games

On the one hand, online games bring people together in complex visual environments created by a marriage of art and technology, and, on the other hand, they construct intricate societies both of players and of non-player characters that are often fractured into competing virtual clans. Social science research methods are appropriate for studying online communities, and the results may inform social science more generally because these are, after all, "real" communities.

8.1 EMERGENT SOCIAL ORGANIZATION

Based on extensive ethnography inside *World of Warcraft*, Nardi and Harris (2006) have classified different levels of social organization that mark collaborations between players. They distinguish two kinds of unstructured collaboration, *strangers in the fight* and *random acts of fun*. An example of the fight classification is buffing a stranger. Some classes of character, such as a priest, have the ability to cast a positive spell on another character, called a *buff*, at the cost of a small amount of mana. If the spell caster is not currently in a battle, this mana replenishes quickly and thus costs the buffer nothing. Some buffs briefly diminish the recipient's health, and some buffs require the recipient to be at a high experience level, so a buffer must exercise some care. However, players very often buff other players they encounter at random, as a gesture of benevolence and an expression of their own competence.

Another "strangers in the fight" example is providing a kill assist when encountering a player locked in combat with a non-player enemy. Here, too, some care is required. In my own experience, I often encounter a player battling a well-matched non-player opponent and feel it would be insulting to the other player to immediately kill the opponent, so I stand and watch. In many MMORPGs, it is easy to monitor the health of both combatants, and if I see that the other player is likely to succeed, I let him or her accomplish the victory alone, which I feel is more honorable. My character stands back so as not to constitute a distraction, and after watching an heroic battle, I will bow at the victor, thus showing respect. However, if the health of the other player becomes imperiled, then a kill assist is warranted, because in all the games there are penalties for being killed. By my observation, many players typically do not follow this somewhat subtle etiquette, and they provide a kill assist even when it is not wanted.

Nardi and Harris also describe structured collaborations with friends and strangers, in four subcategories. First, there are relatively temporary but well-structured small *parties* and larger *raids*, as well as a player's *friends list*. Many quests and instances in essentially all of the MMORPGs require more than one player to complete, and five is the maximum number who can belong to a brief party in *World of Warcraft*. The computer interface lets a player see the health conditions and approximate locations of each of the others, and a special text chat channel opens up for the party members. Raid groups can have as many as 40 members, structured as a collection of parties each with a sub-leader, and I have occasionally participated in raids that were so big they required two or even three raid groups, reaching a hundred total membership. Parties and raid groups can use voice chat as well, although in raids it is often set so that all participants may listen but only sub-group leaders and the chief leader may speak. The leader may also send warning messages that display prominently across the center of each person's computer screen. As Nardi and Harris note, players tend to form friend relationships linking them in pairs who can see when the other person is online and perhaps invite the friend to join a party. Some of these mutually agreed upon friend relationships last a long time, but some are of very short duration, as are parties and raids.

Two other major categories identified by Nardi and Harris are *guilds*, about which there is a very extensive scientific literature, and *battlegrounds* which have not been studied closely. As we shall shortly see in detail, guilds are enduring, structured groups with anywhere from a handful of members, to one or two hundred, to, in rare cases, as many as 5,000 members – noting that members are characters, not players, and a serious player typically has several characters in their favorite guild. Battlegrounds are special instances where two large teams may compete, one representing the Alliance faction and the other the Horde faction, and they can recruit characters from more than one realm (shard) of the game. Since Nardi and Harris did their research, *arena teams* have become very popular, enduring groups the size of small parties that regularly compete in tiny battleground-like instances, rather in the way that amateur basketball teams do, although basketball players rarely "kill" their opponents.

The final major collaboration category identified by Nardi and Harris concerns brief two-person dyads in two subcategories, duels and trades. As the name implies, a *duel* is combat between two players, but they always end with the loser falling on one knee and admitting defeat, rather than being "killed." Duels can often be seen at Goldshire, a short walk from the gate of Stormwind City, although they may happen anyplace. One player challenges another, who is free to accept or reject the challenge, and a tall flag appears to tell others that a duel is in progress. The winner may challenge all comers, which is one reason that a few locations like Goldshire have become traditional dueling sites.

A *trade* is a peaceful economic exchange, in which the user interface ensures that neither party will steal from the other. When one character proposes a trade to another, both see a trade window, which has one side for each character, where the virtual goods or money to be given are placed. Only after both players accept the trade does it take place. A special text chat channel for the local geographic zone is labeled *trade*, and players are encouraged to use it to advertise whatever business they want to do. However, very often players who have no business use the trade channel for ceaseless chattering, and the Barrens local trade chat has become a venue for joking rather than the intended economic behavior.

In a related study, Nardi et al. (2007) showed that the text chat was an effective channel through which players could learn in three different ways: fact finding, developing tactics or strategy, and being socialized to the norms and values that constitute game ethos. Furthermore, they argued, social learning in these games was emotional as well as cognitive. Papargyris and Poulymenakou (2004) argue that players of online multiplayer games learn lessons that can be transferred to real-world organizations, in such areas a teamwork, negotiation, and management of projects.

8.2   EXAMPLES OF GUILDS

Table 8.1 compares three of my typical research characters and their guilds in different worlds, based on information a member of each guild could see in the user interface on September 24, 2009. The first thing to note is that the three guilds, and indeed the three games, are rather similar. One difference is that *Dark Age of Camelot* has an experience level cap of 50, whereas the maximum is 80 in the other two. All three have multiple servers, and characters can interact only if they are on the same server. At this point in time, *World of Warcraft* had 241 North American servers, 112 of which were PvP servers where conflict between players increased the importance of belonging to a supportive guild. *Age of Conan* had 8 North American servers, 4 of them PvP. *Dark Age of Camelot* had effectively five "clusters" of servers, but one of them, Ywain, had over ninety percent of the players. The majority of players had recently moved to Ywain from other clusters that had populations too low to sustain a viable society, and about 4,000 players every evening were rapidly forming new friendships and guilds. Gaheris was the second-most populous server and was distinctive in that the three cultures (Albion, Midgard, and Hibernia) were at peace and could belong to the same guild.

Table 8.1: Typical Characters and Guilds in Three Games.			
	World of Warcraft	Age of Conan	Dark Age of Camelot
Maximum Level	80	80	50
Server	Earthen Ring	Ironspire	Gaheris
Character	Sciencemag	Boadicea	Reitsche
Faction	Horde	none	Midgard
Race	Blood Elf	Cimmerian	Viking
Class	hunter	bear shaman	valkyrie
Level	20	30	35
Guild	Science	Warlords	Legend
Members	333	154	265
Mean Level	27.3	47.6	44.9
Top Level	7.8%	16.2%	74.0%

I created the Science guild myself for the May 2008 scientific conference I organized in *World of Warcraft* with assistance from the magazine *Science* whose website is www.sciencemag.org, so I named the guild master Sciencemag. After the conference, I handed control over to members who wanted to continue, and the guild has survived for over a year. The reason the average member is at a somewhat low level, and only 7.8 percent have reached the top level 80, is that many members are inactive, having joined for sake of the conference. The Warlords exist in a recent and not very popular game, so it is not surprising that few have reached the experience ceiling. At the opposite extreme, the Legend guild is composed overwhelmingly of top level characters because their game was popular when it came out but is now eight years old. Indeed, dedicated *Dark Age of Camelot* players tend to have multiple top-level characters, and many of them own substantial virtual villages in the game, something also possible in *Age of Conan* but not in *World of Warcraft*.

To get a perspective on how characters with different qualities combine to form a guild, Table 8.2 tabulates race versus class for fully 5,042 members of Alea Iacta Est in *World of Warcraft*, who have reached at least level 10 of experience at the beginning of October 2009. This guild had grown substantially since the data on professions cited above were collected a year and a half earlier, and it is one of very largest groups in the games described here. It got its start as an adjunct of the most popular *World of Warcraft* podcast, The Instance, which had transmitted fully 164 professional-quality weekly programs by the time the new data were collected[1]. While not representative in the sense of statistical sampling, I believe this guild is actually the best for research on the culture of *World of Warcraft* because the members are so knowledgeable, and the podcast functions as the news center for the dedicated player community.

Table 8.2: Alea Iacta Est Members in *World of Warcraft*.

Class	Blood Elf	Orc	Tauren	Troll	Undead
Death Knight	12%	21%	13%	9%	12%
Druid	0%	0%	47%	0%	0%
Hunter	14%	30%	11%	25%	0%
Mage	15%	0%	0%	11%	20%
Paladin	28%	0%	0%	0%	0%
Priest	12%	0%	0%	15%	19%
Rogue	8%	5%	0%	11%	15%
Shaman	0%	18%	15%	23%	0%
Warlock	12%	8%	0%	0%	25%
Warrior	0%	17%	14%	5%	9%
Total	100%	100%	100%	100%	100%
Cases	1,980	714	1,082	527	739

There are currently ten races of characters in the game (two more have recently been announced for the third game expansion), and the five listed in Table 8.2 are the ones that belong to the Horde faction. The death knight class, which was added in the second major expansion, is the only one available to characters of all races. Notice that 28 percent of Blood Elves are paladins, and 47 percent of Tauren are Druids, while no other races have characters in this class. Every zero in the table

---

[1] http://www.myextralife.com/wow/

represents a forbidden cell, in which the indicated combination of race and class is not available currently in the game.

Twenty-eight percent of these characters are female characters, and they are distributed across all races and classes. Females are somewhat overrepresented among two non-violent magical classes, priests (13 percent of female characters versus 7 percent of the males) and warlocks (13 percent versus 8). Just 3 percent of female characters are warriors, compared with 9 percent of male characters. By far the most popular race for female characters is the Blood Elves, to which 45 percent of the females belong, compared with 11 percent female among Orcs at the opposite extreme. The Blood Elves are very beautiful, even angelic-looking people, and when a female Blood Elf dances, she duplicates the moves of that popular entertainer, Britney Spears.

Races differ very little in their capabilities, other than in the classes available to them, but their appearance and backstory lore differ greatly. Except for the Orcs and Trolls who start the game in the same zone, each race has a different experience of the first twenty experience levels because it begins in a different area of virtual geography. Priests are the most effective healers, whereas warriors are the most effective "tanks" who directly engage and hold the enemy during combat. Mages and rogues are especially good at inflicting damage on an enemy from a distance, while a warrior holds the foe and a priest heals the warrior. I tend to think that paladins and death knights are good characters for solo play because they combine some of the qualities of warrior and priest. However, hunters and warlocks are also good for solo play because each of them has a secondary avatar that can serve as a tank. It is important to realize that the members of Alea Iacta Est are characters, not players, and each dedicated player tends to have multiple characters that can play different roles in group activities. When a raid or questing party is being formed, one often sees players log off from one character and log back on with a different character whose abilities are better suited to the group challenge.

8.3 QUANTITATIVE RESEARCH ON GUILDS

Many multiplayer games permit the user to create programs, often in the Lua scripting language, that run through the game, so long as the program does not confer a competitive advantage, and a number of researchers have begun using such programs to collect useful data (Ducheneaut et al., 2006). For example, Pittman and Dickey (2007) adapted the existing CensusPlus open source program to collect data on 12,000 *World of Warcraft* characters in 32,000 individual playing sessions over a period of five weeks. CensusPlus queries the interface's "who" routine that lets players look for other players with specified characteristics, then tabulates how many characters in different categories are currently online, and saves the full dataset as a text file. This study chiefly looked at patterns of activity over the hours of the day and across virtual geographic zones, finding that many characters were online only briefly and disproportionately in certain zones. Tarng et al. (2008) did a similar study but with the aim of predicting when players of *World of Warcraft* might cancel their subscriptions, while Feng et al. (2007) used comparable methods to study the varying workload in *EVE Online*. Ideally, one would want to do quantitative research with full access to the data on the host computer, and Kwok and Yeung (2005) showed how this could be done with a text-based gameworld called RockyMud.

Using automatic censuses of characters online at many points in time, Ducheneaut et al. (2007) found that the average size of *World of Warcraft* guilds tended to get larger over a period of months, and that character *churn* (movement between guilds) tended to go down. This suggests that the social structures of games may consolidate over time, and that guilds may serve different functions for players at different levels of experience and with different personal goals.

On the basis of a player interview study, Williams et al. (2006) constructed a typology of *World of Warcraft* guilds. *Social guilds* are numerous but often small collections of friends or family members who enjoy questing together as an extension of their social relationships. In a *PvP guild*, the goal is competing with other PvP guilds in a manner analogous to competition between athletic teams. A *raiding guild* is like a PvP guild but large and dedicated, participating in the very large-scale combats staged on battlegrounds. More problematic, and difficult to study because they seemed to be rare, were *role-playing guilds* that supported members' desires to become their characters. In a quantitative study of guilds of *World of Warcraft* players in Taiwan, Chen et al. (2008) identified five types of guilds in terms of the expertise and dedication of their members: newbie guilds, small but somewhat stable guilds, very stable large guilds, elite guilds composed of high-level players, and mid-level guilds whose progress seemed to have stalled and which declined.

CHAPTER 9

Implications for External Society

Social scientists have long believed that real-world society can be analyzed in terms of a game, and that play is an essential part of becoming human (Von Neumann and Morgenstern, 1944; Huizinga, J., 1949; Winnicott, D., 1971). Long, N. (1958) even argued that local communities could be described as ecologies in which several related games play out simultaneously, such as banking, newspaper publishing, churches, labor unions, construction contractors, manufacturing, and politics. However, one must not rely too heavily upon a metaphor, and researchers will need to be alert to the many ways in which online games are different from other spheres of human experience, the better to understand both (Ducheneaut, N., 2010).

9.1   THE ONLINE GAME PENUMBRA

The first important fact to note about the relationship between multiplayer online games and the surrounding society is that a considerable amount of online interaction takes place around the games but outside them. I call this the *penumbra* of the gaming universe, the blurry edge of its shadow. The more popular a game is, the more heavily populated its penumbra will be, and thus the more diverse and intense the para-game activities will be.

Of course, part of this penumbra is created by the game companies themselves, in the form of spin-off projects. Especially notable are the novels and shorter fiction stories that have been written to flesh out the mythos of a game. The most striking example is "Of Blood and Honor" by Metzen, C. (2002), the man primarily responsible for the lore and storyline in *World of Warcraft*, which tells the tragedy of a strange friendship between the Human aristocrat Tirion Fordring and the Orc warrior Eitrigg, in a manner that contrasts family loyalty against moral principles in a philosophically sophisticated debate. A comparably challenging example is the online novel *Prophet Without Honour* by Tørnquist, R. (2001), one of the creators of *Anarchy Online*. Novelettes can be found on the website of *EVE Online*, and the European distributor of *Dark Age of Camelot* has posted much lore in five languages. Even *Star Wars Galaxies*, based on a mythos for which many novels already existed, was extended in this form (Whitney-Robinson, V., 2004).

Most popular games have their own wikis and other user-created guides. The two most stunning examples concern the most popular MMORPG, *World of Warcraft*: Wowwiki the wiki encyclopedia and WoWHead the tactics-oriented game guide. Wowwiki was originally launched in November 2004, and by September 1 2009, it offered fully 77,187 content pages and 40,184 images, serving and created by 1,530,994 registered users[1]. On that same date, WoWHead offered the official text and user-created instructions for completing fully 8,093 quests. It also provided often detailed descriptions of 1,232 status-conferring achievements, 34,166 virtual items, and 46,565 magical spells. All the games also have forums, where players can ask questions of other players and sometimes get good answers, and amateur websites covering one or another aspect of the game. One of the ways to gain status outside a game but in connection to it is to post proud accomplishments on the web in a manner that is informative to other players, for example, the stunning user-created catalog of spaceships in *EVE Online*[2].

In some cases, fans have modified existing games to add features and content. One educationally relevant example concerns the strategy game *Rome: Total War*, which can be played in a limited multiplayer mode but is usually considered to be s solo-player game in which the user commands Roman legions against the barbarians. Feeling that the barbarians were not depicted with as great historical accuracy as the Romans, an online network of players created a modified version of the game, called *Europa Barbarorum* – "Europe of the Barbarians" – adding content that improved the accuracy and educational interest of the game. Although overshadowed by the great popular success of commercial online multiplayer games, considerable creativity is shown by many networks of enthusiasts who create and modify games following open source principles (Scacchi, W., 2004). As Kow and Nardi (2010) have shown, there exists an active worldwide community of people who program *add-on* or *mod* programs to enhance the user's experience of *World of Warcraft*, deserving of study in its own right.

To emphasize the fact that online role-playing games blend the human person with the computer system, McArthur, V. (2008) has coined the term *ludic cyborg*. While the debate rages about the extent to which people become psychologically immersed in virtual worlds, a very different perspective looks at the way these environments are themselves technically and socially integrated into the surrounding world. This is most obvious in the case of *pervasive LARPs*, live-action role-playing games that are conducted in the real world but utilizing Internet for some of the actions and communications. *Pervasive computing* is a term, especially popular in Europe, for what American computer scientists calls *ubiquitous computing* or *ubicomp*. The idea is that with universal wireless or cellphone connectivity and the convergence of all popular forms of electronic communication into one, people will be playing online games that are integrated into their lives in a variety of ways.

Crabtree and Rodden (2008, p. 481) describe *hybrid ecologies*, "which marry mixed reality environments and ubiquitous computing environments together to bridge the physical-digital divide. Hybrid ecologies are new class of digital ecology that merge multiple environments, physical and digital, together. Collaboration in these emerging environments is characterized by 'fragmented interaction' in that it is mediated by interaction mechanisms that are differentially distributed." Their introductory example is a pervasive game called *Uncle Roy All Around You*, a research-oriented game played in the real world but getting clues over Internet, on a quest to find a particular real-

---

[1]http://www.wowwiki.com/WoWWiki:About
[2]http://www.eveonlineships.com/

world location. Some players are on the street, using mobile technology, whereas others are entirely online and represented by avatars, and both use a kind of geographic information system that tracks movements across the city. Crabtree and Rodden (2008, p. 490) suggest four processes that achieve this hybridization:

- Media spaces LINK physical spaces through digital mediums.

- Mixed reality environments FUSE physical and digital environments.

- Ubiquitous computing environments EMBED the digital into physical environments.

- Hybrid ecologies MERGE multiple environments, physical and digital.

It would be wrong to imagine that these insights are limited to pervasive LARPS or to new kinds of games that might be invented in the future. Lindtner et al. (2008) argue that *World of Warcraft* is already part of a hybrid ecology, based on research looking at how the game is played in China and integrated into people's lives there, with the possibility that different national cultures might be hospitable to different kinds of hybrid ecologies. Notably, many players in China access the game in a kind of game-oriented cybercafé called a *wang ba*, where players often sit next to each other, each operating a computer, as they quest together across virtual continents:

> In the *wang ba*, players used a mix of digital artifacts and software tools, such as external chat clients, in-game chat clients, mobile phone numbers, and virtual characters, as well as resources in the *wang ba* to engage in a rich play experience. The "game" was not simply the software files downloaded on a player's machine or accessed at the *wang ba*; it was, rather, a collage of artifacts and data collectively assembled by its engaged participants. For example, for many players exchange of real life data, such as mobile phone numbers, information about professional careers, and physical location allowed them to express trust in players met online (Lindtner et al., 2008, p. 376).

Examples from western countries are different but numerous. I remember shortly before the Lich King expansion was released in stores, questing in *World of Warcraft* while at home and discovering from the text chat that some of my guildmates were playing on laptops using wireless while waiting in line for the store to open so they could purchase it, naturally socializing with the other players *in* line as well as *on* line.

9.2   WHAT PEOPLE LEARN IN ONLINE GAMES

Over the years, considerable effort has been invested in creating computer games for educational purposes, and today much of the emphasis is on multiplayer games with the hope that students will motivate each other. There are two fundamentally different conceptions of how a game can be educational. First, it can be a delivery vehicle for conventional curriculum, for example, drilling school children in the multiplication table, but there is good reason to doubt that much of the current school curriculum will be worth delivering by whatever means to students whose lives will extend to the very end of the twenty-first century and perhaps beyond. Second, games can teach habits of thought, including strategies for exploration and creativity, whether or not some conventional curriculum is also delivered at the same time.

A good example is *Quest Atlantis*, a well-established multiplayer game designed to help students deepen their comprehension of issues facing our own society by helping the fictional people of Atlantis decide how to deal with a host of social and environmental problems (Barab et al., 2007). After achieving a good deal of success documented in many publications, its creators went a big step further, developing a programming toolkit so teachers and students could create their own quest narratives. This enhancement is based on two principles: "First, employing narrative to stimulate creative work is a valuable and broadly applicable method. Second, creativity is best framed within an active social network. This project characterizes the children's activity in terms uniquely suited to the new millennium: collaborative, distributed, negotiated, and critical"[3].

Based on observational research in *Lineage*, *World of Warcraft*, and *Second Life*, Steinkuehler, C. (2008), (Steinkuehler and Chmiel, 2006) has identified a number of valuable kinds of learning that players may gain even in games that were not designed with educational goals in mind. One example is how the logical styles of thought required for science are exercised when a *World of Warcraft* player decides which abilities from three alternative talent trees to give a particular character. In addition to scientific habits of mind, Steinkuehler suggests five other modes of cognition that player may learn. First, they gain experience in socially distributed cognition, where a network of individuals make discoveries and decisions they could not have made alone, using complex systems of communication. Second, they learn to collaborate to achieve practical goals. Third, they gain skills using specialized forms of language, not unlike those employed in science-based professions but also developing narrative skills. Fourth, handling the games' complex user interfaces and online information resources, their computer literacy improves. Finally, they learn general mechanisms that may lead to success in many real-world contexts, such as what Steinkuehler calls *reciprocal apprenticeship* in which people tutor each other by sharing information and actively debating its meaning.

Playing online multiplayer games may enhance the user's understanding of cultural diversity, both because the games themselves are cultural systems and because other players come from different real-world cultures. A remarkable feature of MMORPGs and other virtual worlds is how international they are. The offices of *World of Warcraft* are in Irvine, California, but it is owned by a transnational corporation headquartered in France, and only about a quarter of the players live in the United States. *Age of Conan* is based on stories written in Texas but was created by a Norwegian company. *Entropia Universe* hails from Sweden, and *EVE Online* is an Icelandic production. Korea is among the most prominent nations producing MMORPGs, and others were created in Japan and China. To the extent that games aim for an international audience, they intentionally blend cultural elements from diverse sources. In so doing, and by using Internet, they bring people together across cultural and national boundaries. I remember one time when I helped attack the Horde city, Or-

---

[3] http://www.nsf.gov/awardsearch/showAward.do?AwardNumber=0855852

grimmar, mentally in *World of Warcraft* but physically in the United States, knowing that the warrior beside me was in Canada, and the married couple leading the charge about twenty feet ahead of us were in England.

The cultural fusion becomes especially interesting when players speak different native languages. Standing in front of a weapon store in *Tabula Rasa*, you would see the sign cycle between English, French, German, and Korean, and you could download patches that would make the non-player characters and user interface employ any of these four languages. Some users of the non-game virtual world, *Second Life*, use automatic language translation systems. I have seen a Brazilian type something into the text chat in Portuguese, after which a bot would immediately render it into rough English, after which the Brazilian with some knowledge of English would make corrections. The Japanese game *Final Fantasy XI* was designed to be played by people who lacked a common language, so it incorporated an extensive list of phrases that could be selected by one member of a team and would display in the various correct languages to other members of the team. Interestingly, the players themselves then developed a set of additional words adapted from various languages, what is technically called a *pidgin*, to supplement the stock phrase list (Nolen, C., 2007). Players who want to improve their facility with one of the world's major languages can now play an online game in that language, so long as they recognize that the vocabulary may not be entirely standard (Rankin et al., 2008).

Like the great classic works of literature, online games draw upon existing culture and influence the player's perception of the real world, for example, serving as a metaphor for resource competition between nations, and often functioning as a political allegory. Some argue that these games support the norms and values of the surrounding culture. For example, Rettberg, S. (2008, p. 20) writes:

> *World of Warcraft* is both a game and a simulation that reinforces the values of Western market-driven economies. The game offers its players a capitalist fairytale in which anyone who works hard and strives enough can rise through society's ranks and acquire great wealth. Moreover, beyond simply representing capitalism as good, *World of Warcraft* serves as a tool to educate its players in a range of behaviors and skills specific to the situation of conducting business in an economy controlled by corporations.

However, it could just as well be said that *World of Warcraft* is explicitly critical of capitalism and of political practices related to it. Many of the quests reveal the elite to be selfish liars, for example, when the rulers of Stormwind send teams of players into the Deadmines to kill Edwin VanCleef, leader of the so-called Defias Bandits. Only when the player brings his severed head back to Stormwind, is it revealed that he was actually the honorable leader of a political movement to seek rights for exploited workers. Another unjust quest requires the assassination of Colonel Kurzen, a renegade military officer who has broken away from Stormwind's Alliance and is living in the Stranglethorn Vale jungle with his private army. He is based on the character Colonel Kurtz in the movie *Apocalypse Now* that satirized the Vietnam War, who was based in turn on Kurtz in Joseph Conrad's novella "Heart of Darkness" that criticized European colonialism in Africa.

Players who are alert to such niceties will experience *World of Warcraft* as a critique of capitalist imperialism, not a defense of it (Langer, J., 2008). Expanding the range of the game's critique, the second expansion late in 2008 added several missions that require torturing prisoners, thus making the player think about proper interrogation techniques in the real-world War on Terror and slaughter peaceful whales while listening to them sing to each other. Since its very beginning in 2004, the game has included many quests incorporating the value of the environmental movement. For example, Figure 9.1 shows two scenes in Windshear Crag, where capitalist gnomes of the Venture Company have chopped down a beautiful forest and made a wasteland, using harmful technologies to fuel their greed. On the left, we see Ozma battling a deforester, with a huge earth-wrecking machine in the background. On the right, Catullus battles a gnome operating an XT-9 logger.

Figure 9.1: Chopping Down Deforesters in *World of Warcraft*.

It is an open question whether most players understand the alegories embedded in many of the games, not to mention the literary references or philosophical principles. Many of the most popular games, including *World of Warcraft*, depict warring societies, none of which have a monopoly on morality. It is entirely possible that these games teach people that loyalty is only valuable when it is expedient, that stealing other people's resources is entirely appropriate, and that the world is a battleground where selfish coalitions compete for survival. A few games lack competing factions of players and teach a different morality, notably *Tabula Rasa* and *Lord of the Rings Online*, but it is a discouraging fact that these idealistic games are less popular.

9.3   RESEARCH OPPORTUNITIES

Many social scientists have begun conducting research in online games and in non-game virtual worlds, on the premise that social behavior is much easier to observe in these computerized environments, yet is comparable to behavior in the outside world (Bainbridge, W., 2007). Whether conceptualized as laboratories or as new regions of the wider human world, they can be used to develop and test theories of human interaction, psychology, and culture. For example, economist Castronova, E. (2005a,b) argues both that an increasing fraction of human economy will take place in virtual environments, so they need to be studied as important phenomena in their own right, and that it can be fruitful to compare results from research in different virtual worlds that follow somewhat different economic principles.

Writing in a medical journal, Lofgren and Fefferman (2007), explained how an unintended disease epidemic in *World of Warcraft* showed how serious epidemiologists could use a virtual world to model the actual spread of infectious diseases. Many games represent disease or poisoning as temporary and often progressive degradation of the character's ability, that under adverse conditions can lead to death. Usually, these virtual diseases are not contagious, but in September 2005, *World of Warcraft* included an infectious disease called "corrupted blood" in a new 20-man raid instance called Zul'Gurub. Given that the teams that enter this instance are fairly large, it must have seemed interesting to allow them to contract a disease from each other, as healer characters attempted to cure their companions even as the infection spread among them. The designers believed they had constructed the instance in such as way that would prevent the infection from spreading outside, but perhaps not enough beta testing had been done to evaluate this hope. Furthermore, while the illness was seldom life-threatening to the level 58-60 characters who could enter the instance, it was often fatal to lower-level characters once it had escaped the confines of the instance.

Leaving Zul'Gurub by the normal route rendered the disease inactive, but apparently the designers had failed to notice that players could teleport out in different ways, and the new programming code did not deactivate the disease for all of them. Also, the hunting animals used by hunter characters could acquire and transmit the disease. To prevent their animals from dying, hunters would often deactivate these secondary avatars, and the code did not cure deactivated animals. Apparently, non-player shopkeepers in the towns and cities also contracted and spread the disease, but they usually were unaffected by it. So, on one level, the epidemic was the result of an innovative game idea, the consequences of which were not fully worked out in the programming. The result was an epidemic that may have infected thousands of players' characters per hour.

Lofgren and Fefferman (2007, p. 627) argue that proper collection of data during a virtual epidemic such as this could explore social factors that operate with real-world plagues, but at far less human cost:

> Whereas the epidemic of Corrupted Blood within *World of Warcraft* was the result of unintended interactions between different elements of the game, it nevertheless shows the potential of such scenarios for the study of infectious disease. One of the major constraints in studies of disease dynamics in animals is that epidemiologists are restricted

largely to observational and retrospective studies. In nearly every case, it is physically impossible, financially prohibitive, or morally reprehensible to create a controlled empirical study where the parameters of the disease are already known before the course of epidemic spread is followed.

A team of researchers at UCLA (Kafai et al., 2007) has actually conducted an experiment by introducing an infectious disease inside the educational children's virtual world, *Whyville*. The symptoms of Whypox were mild: red pimples appeared on the avatars, and they started sneezing "achoo" into the text chat. This was done primarily for educational purposes, as the children could track the spread of the disease, post theories about it, and predict its course. The team used a spectrum of research methods to study what happened:

(1) Log files that recorded all Whyville-based actions of consenting Whyville participants, including information about locations visited, time spent there, and chat content (~70 million data points); (2) online surveys (pre- and post-epidemic) that asked participants (with a combination of multiple choice and open-ended items) about their science and technology interests, understanding of infectious disease, and experiences and preferences in *Whyville* activities; (3) field notes and video recordings of classroom students and after-school club participants while on *Whyville*; (4) face-to-face interviews with selected participants about their *Whyville* interactions, and (5) embedded ethnography that chronicled *Whyville* community life before, during, and after the virtual epidemic.

Like a real disease, Whypox impeded activities. The sneezing in the text chat corrupted some commands and interrupted conversations. The students learned about the course of an epidemic from an information resource that graphed the cases, rising over three days to infect 4,000 characters, then dropping to a low infection rate after most of the population pool had already contracted it. Students tended to generalize excessively from their own personal experience in describing and explaining the course of the disease, rather than thinking scientifically like professional epidemiologists. Their language in describing Whypox in the text chat tended to emphasize symptoms; perhaps, because there were so many different ways they conceptualized other aspects of the disease, such as its transmission modalities, they employed a wide variety of words. Some of the children actually faked the infection, by intentionally sneezing in the text chat. The educational experience seems to have been quite rich as the students shifted from a concern for their own health or illness to an awareness of what was happening to other people to the development of over-arching insights about disease transmission in general.

Bradley and Froomkin (2004) have argued that games and other virtual worlds could be used as laboratories for testing laws and regulations before they are applied in the outside world. Three and four decades ago, real-world social-science experiments were often used to pre-test new government policies before they were enacted on a wide scale, but politicians were disappointed with the results and such studies are far less often done today. The classic example was the 1976 Transitional Aid Research Project (TARP) that at great cost experimented with different programs to assist prisoners released from jail adapt to society (Rossi et al., 1980, 1982; Rossi and Wright, 1984). One pessimistic reading of the findings was that providing short-term financial support and help in finding a job failed to reduce the chance a prisoner would return to a life of crime (Zeisel, H., 1982a,b). The researchers on the project themselves were split, some feeling the study showed that such programs do no good, and others using elaborate statistical techniques to try to find hidden benefits. I can imagine replicating this study inside a multiplayer online game, imprisoning players for being excessively violent, then providing some of them with training and resources to take up a peaceful profession, and seeing if they remain violent. To be sure, we might not want to base real-world government politics entirely on the results of gaming experiments, but they could help strengthen the social science relevant to those policies.

Violence inside games may have implications for violence outside them. In an experimental study that compared new players of *Asheron's Call 2* with a control group, Williams, D. (2006) found some evidence that players became more sensitive to real-world dangers, but only if the dangers were similar to those faced in the game. Massively multiplayer online games put intense pressures on players to join into groups and competing factions, and most of them discourage neutrality in the face of social conflict (Medler, B., 2008). Logically enough, the game designers think that conflict builds group loyalty, and group loyalty commits the player to the particular game, rather than hopping from one to another as soon as each character reaches the maximum experience level. The social scientific study most relevant to this issue is actually a very old one, the famous Robber's Cave Experiment carried out by a team headed by Sherif et al. (1988). Twenty-two boys attended a special summer camp in 1954, where they were divided into two competing groups that called themselves Rattlers and Eagles and developed strong in-group solidarity and out-group hostility by competing intensely against each other.

Multiplayer online games can become laboratories where humanity experiments with new norms, values, and institutions that might later be transferred to the outside world. Whether these innovations will be new forms of conflict or cooperation remains to be seen. Castronova, E. (2007) has suggested that the economic systems of popular games may change people's sense of justice in the real world, for example, causing them to reject inheritance of wealth on the principle that everybody should start the game of life with the same resources.

The quests in these games could enhance the wider human quest for utopia, as one of them explicitly claims: "The objective of *A Tale in the Desert* is to build the ideal civilization by perfecting the Seven Disciplines of Man, with each discipline containing seven tests"[4]. Many of the forty-nine tests require people to cooperate, but so do many of the quests in other games, whose guilds prototype communities of the future. At the risk of ending this lecture about fantasies on an especially fanciful note, these online multiplayer games may be *etopias* – electronic utopias that have the potential to be the proving grounds for real-world social innovation and are already meeting places for real-world subcultures and social movements (Bainbridge, W., 2009).

---

[4] http://atitd.org/wiki/tale4/Tests

Bibliography

Abbott, H. Porter. 2003. "Unnarratable Knowledge: The Difficulty of Understanding Evolution by Natural Selection." Pp. 143–162 in *Narrative Theory and the Cognitive Sciences*, edited by David Herman. Stanford, California: CSLI Publications. 1.3

Abbott, H. Porter. 2008. *The Cambridge Introduction to Narrative*. New York: Cambridge University Press. 1.3

Achterbosch, L., Robyn Pierce, and Gregory Simmons. 2007. "Massively Multiplayer Online Role-Playing Games: The Past, Present, and Future," *Computers in Entertainment* 5(4). 1.4, 3

Adorno, T., Else Frenkel-Brunswik, Daniel Levinson, and Nevitt Sanford. 1950. *The Authoritarian Personality*. New York: Harper. 5.2

Aggarwal, S., Justin Christofoli, Sarit Mukherjee, and Sampath Rangarajan. 2006. "Authority Assignment in Distributed Multi-Player Proxy-Based Games." In Proceedings of 5th ACM SIGCOMM Workshop on Network and System Support for Games. New York: ACM. DOI: 10.1145/1230040.1230068 3.1

Arya, Ali, and Steve Di Paola. 2007. "Multispace Behavioral Model for Face-Based Affective Social Agents," *EURASIP Journal on Image and Video Processing*, article 48757. DOI: 10.1155/2007/48757 5.4

Bainbridge, William Sims. 1986. *Dimensions of Science Fiction*. Cambridge, Massachusetts: Harvard University Press. 2.5

Bainbridge, William Sims. 2007. "The Scientific Research Potential of Virtual Worlds," *Science*, 317 (27 July): 472–476. DOI: 10.1126/science.1146930 9.3

Bainbridge, William Sims. 2009. "Etopia," *Networker* 13(1): 36–35. DOI: 10.1145/1516035.1516045 9.3

Bainbridge, William Sims. 2010a. "Science, Technology and Reality in *The Matrix Online* and *Tabula Rasa*." In *Online Worlds*, edited by William Sims Bainbridge. Guildford, Surrey, England: Springer. 1.2

Bainbridge, William Sims. 2010b. *The Warcraft Civilization*. Cambridge, Massachusetts: MIT Press. 1

Bainbridge, William Sims. 2010c. "When Virtual Worlds Expand." In *Online Worlds*, edited by William Sims Bainbridge. Guildford, Surrey, England: Springer. 1, 4.2

Bainbridge, William Sims, and Wilma Alice Bainbridge. 2007a. "Electronic Game Research Methodologies: Studying Religious Implications," *Review of Religious Research* 49: 35–53. 2.4

Bainbridge, Wilma Alice, and William Sims Bainbridge. 2007b. "Creative Uses of Software Errors: Glitches and Cheats," *Social Science Computer Review* 25: 61–77. DOI: 10.1177/0894439306289510 3.3

Barab, Sasha, Tyler Dodge, Hakan Tuzun, Kirk Job-Sluder, Craig Jackson, Anna Arici, Laura Job-Sluder, Robert Carteaux, Jr., Jo Gilbertson, and Conan Heiselt. 2007. "The Quest Atlantis Project: A Socially-Responsive Play Space for Learning." Pp. 159-186 in *The Educational Design and Use of Simulation Computer Games*, edited by B. E. Shelton and D. Wiley. Rotterdam, The Netherlands: Sense Publishers. 9.2

Bardzell, Shaowen, Jeffrey Bardzell, Tyler Pace, and Kayce Reed. 2008. "Blissfully Productive: Grouping and Cooperation in World of Warcraft Instance Runs." Pp. 357-360 in *Proceedings of the ACM 2008 Conference on Computer Supported Cooperative Work*. New York: ACM. DOI: 10.1145/1460563.1460621 4.2

Barnett, Jane , Mark Coulson, and Nigel Foreman. 2010. "Examining Player Anger in World of Warcraft." In *Online Worlds*, edited by William Sims Bainbridge. Guildford, Surrey, England: Springer. 4.2

Barr, Pippin, Robert Biddle, and Judy Brown. 2006. "Changing the Virtual Self: Avatar Transformations in Popular Games." Pp. 83-90 in *Proceedings of the 3rd Australasian Conference on Interactive Entertainment*. Perth, Western Australia, Australia: Murdoch University. 6.2

Bartle, Richard A. 1996. "Hearts, Clubs, Diamonds, Spades: Players Who Suit MUDs," *Journal of MUD Research* 1; online at
http://www.brandeis.edu/pubs/jove/HTML/v1/bartle.html;
retrieved, November 15, 2008. 5.2

Bartle, Richard A. 2004. *Designing Virtual Worlds*. Indianapolis, Indiana: New Riders. 5.2

Baudrillard, Jean. 1994. *Simulacra and Simulation*. Ann Arbor, Michigan: University of Michigan Press. 1.2

Bedman (aka Captain Stack). 2007. "The Matrix Online for PC: Windows;"
http://www.gamefaqs.com/computer/doswin/file/931849/35989 5.2

Bell, Daniel (ed.). 1963. *The Radical Right*. Garden City, New York: Doubleday. 5.2

Beskow, Paul B., Knut-Helge Vik, Pål Halvorsen, and Carsten Griwodz. 2008. "Latency Reduction by Dynamic Core Selection and Partial Migration of Game State." Pp. 79-84 in *Proceedings of the 7th ACM SIGCOMM Workshop on Network and System Support for Games*. New York: ACM. DOI: 10.1145/1517494.1517511 3.2

Bessiere, Katherine, Fleming Seay, and Sara Kiesler. 2007. "The Ideal Elf: Identity Exploration in *World of Warcraft*." *CyberPsychology and Behavior*, 10: 53-535. 6.2

Blinka, Lukas. 2008. "The Relationship of Players to their Avatars in MMORPGs: Differences between Adolescents, Emerging Adults and Adults," *Cyberpsychology: Journal of Psychosocial Research on Cyberspace*, 1, online at
http://www.cyberpsychology.eu/view.php?cisloclanku=2008060901;
retrieved November 15, 2008. 6.2

Bohannon, John. 2008a. "Scientists Invade Azeroth," *Science*, 320:1592. 3.1

Bohannon, John. 2008b. "Slaying Monsters for Science," online version of *Science*,
http://www.sciencemag.org/cgi/content/full/320/5883/1592c,
retrieved November 19, 2008. 3.1

Bosser, Anne-Gwenn. 2004. "Massively Multi-Player Games: Matching Game Design with Technical Design." Pp. 263-268 in *Proceedings of the 2004 ACM SIGCHI International Conference on Advances in Computer Entertainment Technology*. New York: ACM. DOI: 10.1145/1067343.1067378 3.1

Bradley, Caroline, and A. Michael Froomkin. 2004. "Virtual Worlds, Real Rules," *New York Law School Law Review*, 49:103-146. 9.3

Browning, David, Steven Stanley, Michael Fryer, and Nicola J. Bidwell. 2006. "Emplacing Experience." Pp. 96-103 in *Proceedings of the 2006 International Conference on Game Research and Development*. Perth, Western Australia: Murdoch University. 3.3

Castronova, Edward. 2003. "Network Technology, Markets, and the Growth of Synthetic Worlds." Pp. 121-134 in *Proceedings of the 2nd Workshop on Network and System Support for Games*. New York: ACM. DOI: 10.1145/963900.963912 2

Castronova, Edward. 2005a. "On the Research Value of Large Games: Natural Experiments in Norrath and Camelot," CESifo Working Paper Series No. 1621, Indiana University Bloomington. DOI: 10.1177/1555412006286686 9.3

Castronova, Edward. 2005b. *Synthetic Worlds: The Business and Culture of Online Games*. Chicago: University of Chicago Press. 9.3

Castronova, Edward. 2007. *Exodus to the Virtual World: How Online Fun is Changing Reality*. New York: Palgrave Macmillan. 9.3

Catullus. 2008. "Letter to a Supernatural Being." Pp. 247-255 in *Human Futures: Art in and Age of Uncertainty*, edited by Andy Miah. Liverpool, England: Liverpool University Press. 6.1

Chen, Chien-Hsun, Chuen-Tsai Sun, and Jilung Hsieh. 2008. "Player Guild Dynamics and Evolution in Massively Multiplayer Online Games," *CyberPsychology and Behavior*, 11:293-301. DOI: 10.1089/cpb.2007.0066 8.3

Chen, Kuan-Ta, Chun-Ying Huang, Polly Huang, and Chin-Laung Lei. 2006. "An Empirical Evaluation of TCP Performance in Online Games." *Proceedings of the 2006 ACM SIGCHI International Conference on Advances in Computer Entertainment Technology*. New York: ACM. DOI: 10.1145/1178823.1178830 3.1

Chen, Vivian Hsueh-hua, Henry Been-Lirn Duh, and Hong Renyi. 2008. "The Changing Dynamic of Social Interaction in World of Warcraft: The Impacts of Game Feature Change." Pp. 356-359 in *Proceedings of the 2008 International Conference on Advances in Computer Entertainment Technology*. New York: ACM. DOI: 10.1145/1501750.1501834 4.2

Cikic, Sabine, Sven Grottke, Fritz Lehmann-Grube, and Jan Sablatnig. 2008. "Cheat Prevention and Analysis in Online Virtual Worlds." In *Proceedings of the 1st International Conference on Forensic Applications and Techniques in Telecommunications, Information, and Multimedia*. New York: ACM. 4.2

Cornett, Steve. 2004. "The Usability of Massively Multiplayer Online Roleplaying Games: Designing for New Users." Pp. 703-710 in *Proceedings of the SIGCHI Conference on Human Factors in Computing Systems*. New York: ACM. DOI: 10.1145/985692.985781 3.3

Crabtree, Andy, and Tom Rodden. 2008. "Hybrid Ecologies: Understanding Cooperative Interaction in Emerging Physical-Digital Environments." *Personal and Ubiquitous Computing*, 12:481–493. DOI: 10.1007/s00779-007-0142-7 9.1

Craft, Ashley John. 2007. "Sin in Cyber-Eden: Understanding the Metaphysics and Morals of Virtual Worlds," *Ethics and Information Technology*, 9:205-217. DOI: 10.1007/s10676-007-9144-4 4.1

De Camp, L. Sprague, Catherine Crook de Camp, and Jane Whittington Griffin. 1983. *Dark Valley Destiny: The Life of Robert E. Howard*. New York: Bluejay. 2.3

Dibbell, Julian. 2007. "The Life of the Chinese Gold Farmer," *New York Times* online, June 17, 2007; http://www.nytimes.com/2007/06/17/magazine/17lootfarmers-t.html 4.4

Ducheneaut, Nicolas. 2010. "Massively Multiplayer Online Games as Living Laboratories: Opportunities and Pitfalls." In *Online Worlds*, edited by William Sims Bainbridge. Guildford, Surrey, England: Springer. 9

Ducheneaut, Nicolas, and Robert J. Moore. 2004. "The Social Side of Gaming: A Study of Interaction Patterns in a Massively Multiplayer Online Game." Pp. 360-369 in *Proceedings of the 2004 ACM Conference on Computer Supported Cooperative Work*. New York: ACM. DOI: 10.1145/1031607.1031667 2.5

Ducheneaut, Nicolas, Robert J. Moore, and Eric Nickell. 2007. "Virtual 'Third Places:' A Case Study of Sociability in Massively Multiplayer Games," *Computer Supported Cooperative Work* 16:129-166. DOI: 10.1007/s10606-007-9041-8 2.5

Ducheneaut, Nicolas, Nick Yee, Eric Nickell, and Robert J. Moore. 2006. "Building an MMO With Mass Appeal: A Look at Gameplay in World of Warcraft," *Games and Culture* 1:281-317. DOI: 10.1177/1555412006292613 8.3

Ducheneaut, Nicolas, Nick Yee, Eric Nickell, and Robert J. Moore. 2007. "The Life and Death of Online Gaming Communities: A Look at Guilds in *World of Warcraft*." Pp. 839-848 in *Proceedings of the SIGCHI Conference on Human Factors in Computing Systems*. New York: ACM. 8.3

Ducheneaut, Nicolas, Ming-Hui Wen, Nicholas Yee, and Greg Wadley. 2009. "Body and Mind: A Study of Avatar Personalization in Three Virtual Worlds." Pp. 1151-1160 in *Proceedings of the 27th International Conference on Human Factors in Computing Systems*. New York: ACM. DOI: 10.1145/1518701.1518877 6.2

Durkheim, Emile. 1933. *The Division of Labor in Society*. New York: Free Press. 7.3

Dyck, Jeff, Carl Gutwin, T.C. Nicholas Graham, and David Pinelle. 2007. "Beyond the LAN: Techniques from Network Games for Improving Groupware Performance." Pp. 291-300 in Proceedings of GROUP'07. New York: ACM. DOI: 10.1145/1316624.1316669 3.1

Feng, Wu-chang, David Brandt, and Debanjan Saha. 2007. "A Long-term Study of a Popular MMORPG." Pp. 19-24 in *Proceedings of the 6th ACM SIGCOMM Workshop on Network and System Support for Games*. New York: ACM. 8.3

Foo, Chek Yang, and Elina M.I. Koivisto. 2004. "Defining Grief Play in MMORPGs: Player and Developer Perceptions." Pp. 245-250 in *Proceedings of the 2004 ACM SIGCHI International Conference on Advances in Computer Entertainment Technology*. New York: ACM. DOI: 10.1145/1067343.1067375 4.2

Frasca, Gonzalo. 2003. "Simulation versus Narrative: Introduction to Ludoloogy." Pp. 221-235 in *The Video Game Theory Reader*, edited by Mark J.P. Wolf and Bernard Perron. New York: Routledge.

Freud, Sigmund. 1930. *Civilization and its Discontents*. New York: Cape and Smith.

Fritsch, Tobias, Benjamin Voigt, and Jochen Schiller. 2006. "Distribution of Online Hardcore Player Behavior: (How Hardcore Are You?)." *Proceedings of 5th ACM SIGCOMM Workshop on Network and System Support for Games*. New York: ACM. DOI: 10.1145/1230040.1230082 3.3

Fritsch, Tobias, Jochen Schiller, and Benjamin Voigt. 2007. "Personal Behavior and Virtual Fragmentation." Pp. 60-63 in *Proceedings of the International Conference on Advances in Computer Entertainment Technology*. New York: ACM. DOI: 10.1145/1255047.1255059 3.3

Fron, Janine, Tracy Fullerton, Jacquelyn Ford Morie, and Celia Pearce (aka Ludica). 2007. "Playing Dress-Up: Costume, roleplay and imagination." *Philosophy of Computer Games Online Proceedings*; http://lcc.gatech.edu/~{}cpearce3/PearcePubs/LudicaDress-Up.pdf 6.2

Gordon, Andrew. 1995. "Star Wars: A Myth for Our Time." Pp. 73-82 in *Screening the Sacred: Religion, Myth and Ideology in Popular American Film*, edited by Joel W. Martin and Conrad E. Ostwalt. Boulder, Colorado: Westview Press. 2.5

Grimes, Sara M. 2006. "Online Multiplayer Games: A Virtual Space for Intellectual Property Debates?" *New Media and Society* 8:969-990. DOI: 10.1177/1461444806069651 4.4

Griwodz , Carsten, and Pål Halvorsen. 2006. "The Fun of Using TCP for an MMORP." In *Proceedings of the 2006 International Workshop on Network and Operating Systems Support for Digital Audio and Video*. New York: ACM. DOI: 10.1145/1378191.1378193 3.1

Gygax, Gary. 1979. *Advanced Dungeons and Dragons, Dungeon Masters Guide*. New York: TSR/Random House. 2.5

Halloran, John, Geraldine Fitzpatrick, Yvonne Rogers, and Paul Marshall. 2004. "Does It Matter if You Don't Know Who's Talking?: Multiplayer Gaming with Voiceover IP." Pp. 1215-1218 in *Extended Abstracts of CHI '04 Conference on Human Factors in Computing Systems*. New York: ACM. DOI: 10.1145/985921.986027 3.3

Heise, David R. 2004. "Enculturating Agents With Expressive Role Behavior." Pp. 127-142 in *Agent Culture: Human-Agent Interaction in a Multicultural World*. Mahwah, New Jersey: Erlbaum. 5.4

Holsapple, Clyde W., and Jiming Wu. 2007. "User Acceptance of Virtual Worlds: The Hedonic Framework," *DATA BASE for Advances in Information Systems* 38:86-89. DOI: 10.1145/1314234.1314250 5.2

Homans, George C. 1950. *The Human Group*. New York: Harcourt, Brace. 7.3

Huh, Searle, and Dmitri Williams. 2010. "Dude Looks Like a Lady: Gender Swapping in an Online Game." In *Online Worlds*, edited by William Sims Bainbridge. Guildford, Surrey, England: Springer. 6.2

Huizinga, Johan. 1949. *Homo Ludens: A Study of the Play-Element in Culture*. London: Routledge and Kegan Paul. 9

Humphreys, Sal. 2009. "Norrath: New Forms, Old Institutions." *Game Studies* 9(1); http://gamestudies.org/0901/articles/humphreys 4.4

Hussain, Zaheer, and Mark D. Griffiths. 2008. "Gender Swapping and Socializing in Cyberspace: An Exploratory Study," *CyberPsychology and Behavior* 11:47-53. DOI: 10.1089/cpb.2007.0020 6.2

Jensen-Campbell, Lauri A., Jennifer M. Knack, Amy M. Waldrip, and Shaun D. Campbell. 2007. "Do Big Five Personality Traits Associated with Self-control Influence the Regulation of Anger and Aggression?" *Journal of Research in Personality*, 41: 403–424. DOI: 10.1016/j.jrp.2006.05.001 5.1

Jensen-Campbell, Lauri A., and Kenya T. Malcolm. 2007. "The Importance of Conscientiousness in Adolescent Interpersonal Relationships," *Personality and Social Psychology Bulletin*, 33: 368-383. DOI: 10.1177/0146167206296104 5.1

Jonsson, Staffan, Markus Montola, Annika Waern, and Martin Ericsson. 2006. " Prosopopeia: Experiences from a Pervasive LARP." In *Proceedings of the 2006 ACM SIGCHI International Conference on Advances in Computer Entertainment Technology*. New York: ACM DOI: 10.1145/1178823.1178850 1.1

Jørgensen, Kristine. 2008. "Audio and Gameplay: An Analysis of PvP Battlegrounds in World of Warcraft," *Game Studies* 8(2);
http://gamestudies.org/0802/articles/jorgensen 3.3

Kafai, Yasmin B., David Feldon, Deborah Fields, Michael Giang, and Maria Quintero. 2007. "Life in the Time of Whypox: A Virtual Epidemic as a Community Event." Pp. 171-190 in *Communities and Technologies*, edited by C. Steinfield, B. Pentland, M. Ackerman, and N. Contractor. New York: Springer. 9.3

Kinnard, Roy. 1988. "The Flash Gordon Serials," *Films in Review* 39(4):194-203. 2.5

Klastrup, Lisbeth. 2006. "Death Matters: Understanding Gameworld Experiences." In *Proceedings of the 2006 ACM SIGCHI International Conference on Advances in Computer Entertainment Technology*. New York: ACM. DOI: 10.1145/1178823.1178859 6.4

Klastrup, Lisbeth. 2008. "What Makes World of Warcraft a World? A Note on Death and Dying." Pp. 143-166 in *Digital Culture, Play and Identity: A World of Warcraft Reader*, edited by Hilde G. Corneliussen and Jill Walker Rettberg. Cambridge, Massachusetts: MIT Press. 6.4

Klastrup, Lisbeth. 2009. "The Worldness of *EverQuest*: Exploring a 21st Century Fiction," *Game Studies* 9(1);
http://gamestudies.org/0901/articles/klastrup 1.3

Kow, Yong Ming, and Bonnie Nardi. 2010. "Culture and Creativity: World of Warcraft Modding in China and the U.S." In *Online Worlds*, edited by William Sims Bainbridge. Guildford, Surrey, England: Springer. 9.1

Krzywinska, Tanya. 2006. "Blood Sythes, Festivals, Quests, and Backstories," *Games and Culture* 1:383-396. 2

Kshirsagar, Sumedha, and Nadia Magnenat-Thalmann. 2002. "A Multilayer Personality Model." Pp. 107-115 in *Proceedings of the Symposium on Smart Graphics*. New York: ACM. DOI: 10.1145/569005.569021 5.4

Kwok, Michael, and Gary Yeung. 2005. "Characterization of User Behavior in a Multi-Player Online Game." Pp. 69-74 in *Proceedings of the 2005 ACM SIGCHI International Conference on Advances in Computer Entertainment Technology*. New York: ACM. DOI: 10.1145/1178477.1178486 8.3

Langer, Jessica. 2008. "The Familiar and the Foreign: Playing (Post)Colonialism in World of Warcraft." Pp. 87-108 in *Digital Culture, Play and Identity: A World of Warcraft Reader*, edited by Hilde G. Corneliussen and Jill Walker Rettberg. Cambridge, Massachusetts: MIT Press. 9.2

Lastowka, Greg. 2009. "Planes of Power: EverQuest as Text, Game and Community." *Game Studies* 9(1); http://gamestudies.org/0901/articles/lastowka 4.4

Li, Kang, Shanshan Ding, Doug McCreary, and Steve Webb. 2004. "Analysis of State Exposure Control to Prevent Cheating in Online Games." Pp. 140-145 in *Proceedings of the 14th International Workshop on Network and Operating Systems Support for Digital Audio and Video*. New York: ACM. DOI: 10.1145/1005847.1005878 4.2

Lindtner, Silvia, Bonnie Nardi, Yang Wang, Scott Mainwaring, He Jing, Wenjing Liang. 2008. "A Hybrid Cultural Ecology: *World of Warcraft* in China." Pp. 371-382 in Proceedings of the ACM 2008 Conference on Computer Supported Cooperative Work. New York: ACM. DOI: 10.1145/1460563.1460624 9.1

Lindzey, Gardner, and Elliot Aronson (eds.). 1968. *The Handbook of Social Psychology*. Reading, Massachusetts: Addison-Wesley. 5.1

Lipset, Seymour Martin, and Earl Raab. 1970. *The Politics of Unreason: Right-wing Extremism in America*. New York: Harper and Row. 5.2

Lofgren, Eric T., and Nina H. Fefferman. 2007. "The Untapped Potential of Virtual Game Worlds to Shed Light on Real World Epidemics," *The Lancet Infectious Diseases*, 7: 625-629. DOI: 10.1016/S1473-3099(07)70212-8 9.3

Long, Norton E. 1958. "The Local Community as an Ecology of Games." *American Journal of Sociology* 64: 251-261. DOI: 10.1086/222468 9

Lu, Fengyun, Simon Parkin, and Graham Morgan. 2006. "Load Balancing for Massively Multiplayer Online Games." *Proceedings of 5th ACM SIGCOMM Workshop on Network and System Support for Games*. New York: ACM. DOI: 10.1145/1230040.1230064 3.2

Lummis, Michael, and Edwin Kern. 2006. *World of Warcraft Master Guide*. Indianapolis, Indiana: BradyGAMES/DK. 1.3

Lupoff, Richard A. 1976. *Edgar Rice Burroughs and the Martian Vision*. Westminster, Maryland: Mirage Press. 2.5

Maher, Mary Lou, Kathryn Merrick, and Owen Macindoe. 2005. "Can Designs Themselves Be Creative?" Pp. 11-135 in *Proceedings of the Sixth International Roundtable Conference on Computational and Cognitive Models of Creative Design*, Heron Island, Australia. 1.4

Massey, Douglas S. 2002. "A Brief History of Human Society: The Origin and Role of Emotion in Social Life." *American Sociological Review* 61:1-29. 2.3

McArthur, Victoria. 2008. "World of Warcraft as a Ludic Cyborg." Pp. 264-265 in *Proceedings of the 2008 Conference on Future Play: Research, Play, Share*. New York: ACM. DOI: 10.1145/1496984.1497046 9.1

McClelland, David C. 1961. *The Achieving Society*. Princeton, New Jersey: Van Nostrand. 5.2

McCrae, Robert R., and Paul T. Costa. 1989. "Reinterpreting the Myers-Briggs Type Indicator from the Perspective of the Five-Factor Model of Personality," *Journal of Personality* 57:17-40. DOI: 10.1111/j.1467-6494.1989.tb00759.x 5.3

McCrae, Robert R., and Paul T. Costa. 1996. "Toward a New Generation of Personality Theories: Theoretical Contexts for the Five-Factor Model." Pp. 51-87 in *The Five-Factor Model of Personality: Theoretical Perspectives*, edited by Jerry S. Wiggins. New York: Guilford Press. 5.1

McCubbin, Chris. 2005. *The Matrix Online: Prima Official Game Guide*. Roseville, California: Prima Games. 1.2

McCubbin, Chris, David Ladyman, and Tuesday Frase (eds.). 2005. *Star Wars Galaxies: The Total Experience*. Roseville, California: Prima Games. 7.1

McGregor, Georgia Leigh. 2006. "Architecture, Space and Gameplay in *World of Warcraft* and *Battle for Middle Earth 2*. Pp. 69-76 in *Proceedings of the 2006 International Conference on Game Research and Development*. Perth, Australia: Murdoch University. 3.3

Medler, Ben. 2008. "Views From Atop the Fence: Neutrality in Games." Pp. 81-88 in *Proceedings of the 2008 ACM SIGGRAPH Symposium on Video Games*. New York: ACM. DOI: 10.1145/1401843.1401860 9.3

Merrick, Kathryn, Mary Lou Maher. 2006. "Motivated Reinforcement Learning for Non-Player Characters in Persistent Computer Game Worlds." In *Proceedings of the 2006 ACM SIGCHI International Conference on Advances in computer Entertainment Technology*. New York: ACM. DOI: 10.1145/1178823.1178828 1.4

Metzen, Chris. 2002. "Of Blood and Honor." Pp. 545-613 in *Warcraft Archive*. New York: Pocket Books. 9.1

Moore, Robert J., Nicolas Ducheneaut, and Eric Nickell. 2007. "Doing Virtually Nothing: Awareness and Accountability in Massively Multiplayer Online Worlds," *Computer Supported Cooperative Work* 16:265-305. DOI: 10.1007/s10606-006-9021-4 3.3

Moriarty, Christopher, and Avelino J. Gonzalez. 2009. "Learning Human Behavior from Observation for Gaming Applications." *Proceedings of the 22nd International Florida Artificial Intelligence Research Society Conference (FLAIRS-2009)*, Sanibel Island, FL, May 19-21, 2009. 1.4

Murray, Henry A. 1981. *Endeavors in Psychology: Selections from the Personology of Henry A. Murray*. New York: Harper and Row. 5.3

Mylonas, Eric. 2005. *Dark Age of Camelot: Epic Edition*. Roseville, California: Prima Games. 2.2

Nardi, Bonnie. 2010. *My Life as a Night Elf Priest: An Anthropological Account of World of Warcraft*. Ann Arbor: University of Michigan Press. 1

Nardi, Bonnie, and Justin Harris. 2006. "Strangers and Friends: Collaborative Play in *World of Warcraft*." Pp. 149-158 in *Proceedings of the 2006 20th Anniversary Conference on Computer Supported Cooperative Work*. New York: ACM. 8.1

Nardi, Bonnie A., Stella Ly, and Justin Harris. 2007. "Learning Conversations in World of Warcraft." In *Proceedings of the 40th Annual Hawaii International Conference on System Sciences*. Washington, DC: IEEE Computer Society. DOI: 10.1109/HICSS.2007.321 8.1

Nolen, Chelsea Winter. 2007. "Virtual Pluralities: Cultural Pluralism in a Massively Multiplayer Online Role-Playing Game." Unpublished senior thesis. St. Louis, Missouri: Washington University. 9.2

Osgood, Charles E., George J. Suci, and Percy H. Tannenbaum. 1957. *The Measurement of Meaning*. Urbana: University of Illinois Press. 5.4

Osgood, Charles E., William H. May, and Murray S. Miron. 1975. Cross-Cultural Universals of Affective Meaning. Urbana: University of Illinois Press.

Pangburn, Weaver. 1922. "The Worker's Leisure and His Individuality," *American Journal of Sociology*, 27: 433-441. DOI: 10.1086/213375 6

Pantel, Lothar, and Lars C. Wolf. 2002. "On the Impact of Delay on Real-Time Multiplayer Games." Pp. 23-29 in *Proceedings of the 12th International Workshop on Network and Operating Systems Support for Digital Audio and Video*. New York: ACM. DOI: 10.1145/507670.507674 3.1

Papargyris, Anthony, and Angeliki Poulymenakou. 2004. "Learning to Fly in Persistent Digital Worlds: The Case of Massively Multiplayer Online Role Playing Games," *SIGGROUP Bulletin* 25:41-49. DOI: 10.1145/1067699.1067706 8.1

Pearce, Celia. 2010. "The Diasporic Game Community: Trans-Ludic Cultures and Latitudinal Research Across Multiple Games and Virtual Worlds." In *Online Worlds*, edited by William Sims Bainbridge. Guildford, Surrey, England: Springer. 1.2

Peter, Christian, and Russell Beale (eds.). 2008. *Affect and Emotion in Human-Computer Interaction*. Berlin: Springer. DOI: 10.1007/978-3-540-85099-1 2.3

Pittman, Daniel, and Chris Gauthier Dickey. 2007. "A Measurement Study of Virtual Populations in Massively Multiplayer Online Games." Pp. 25-30 in *Proceedings of the 6th ACM SIGCOMM Workshop on Network and System Support for Games*. New York: ACM. DOI: 10.1145/1326257.1326262 8.3

Picard, Rosalind W. 1997. *Affective Computing*. Cambridge, Massachusetts: MIT Press. 2.3

Porges, Irwin. 1975. *Edgar Rice Burroughs: The Man who Created Tarzan*. Provo, Utah: Brigham Young University Press. 2.5

Prensky, Marc. 2001. *Digital Game-based Learning*. New York: McGraw-Hill. 1.3

Rankin, Yolanda A., McKenzie McNeal, Marcus W. Shute, and Bruce Gooch. 2008. "User Centered Game Design: Evaluating Massive Multiplayer Online Role Playing Games for Second Language Acquisition." Pp. 43-49 in *Proceedings of the 2008 ACM SIGGRAPH Symposium on Video Games*. New York: ACM. DOI: 10.1145/1401843.1401851 9.2

Robinett, Warren. 2003. "Foreword." Pp. vi-xix in *The Video Game Theory Reader*, edited by Mark J.P. Wolf and Bernard Perron. New York: Routledge. 4.2

Rossi, Peter H., and James D. Wright. 1984. "Evaluation Research: An Assessment," *Annual Review of Sociology* 10:331-352. DOI: 10.1146/annurev.so.10.080184.001555 9.3

Rettberg, Scott. 2008. "Corporate Ideology in World of Warcraft." Pp. 19-38 in *Digital Culture, Play, and Identity: A World of Warcraft Reader*, edited by Hilde G. Corneliussen and Jill Walker Rettberg. Cambridge, Massachusetts: MIT Press. 9.2

Rossi, Peter H., Richard A. Berk, and Kenneth J. Lenihan. 1980. *Money, Work, and Crime*. New York: Academic Press. 9.3

Rossi, Peter H., Richard A. Berk, and Kenneth J. Lenihan. 1982. "Saying it Wrong with Figures," *American Journal of Sociology* 88:390-393. DOI: 10.1086/227677 9.3

Rouse, Richard. 2001. *Game Design: Theory and Practice*. Plano, Texas: Woodware. 1.3

Ryan, Marie-Laure. 2001. "Beyond Myth and Metaphor: The Case of Narrative in Digital Media." *Game Studies* 1 (July); http://www.gamestudies.org/0101/ryan/ 6.1

Rymaszewski, Michael, Wagner James Au, Mark Wallace, Catherine Winters, Cory Ondrejka, and Benjamin Batstone-Cunningham. 2007. *Second Life: The Official Guide*. Hoboken, New Jersey: Wiley. 1.1

Scacchi, Walt. 2004. "Free and Open Source Development Practices in the Game Community," *IEEE Software* 21(1):59-66. DOI: 10.1109/MS.2004.1259221 9.1

Schultze, Ulrike, and Matthew Michael Leahy. 2009. "The Avatar-Self Relationship: Enacting Presence in Second Life." In *Proceedings of the Thirtieth International Conference on Information Systems*. Atlanta, Georgia: Association for Information Systems. 6.2

Schütz, Alfred. 1971. "On Multiple Realities." Pp. 207-259 in *Collected Papers*. The Hague, Netherlands: Nijhoff. 5.3

Sears, Andrew, Jonathan Lazar, Ant Ozok, and Gabriele Meiselwitz. 2008. "Human-Centered Computing: Defining a Research Agenda." *International Journal of Human-Computer Interaction* 24:2-16. DOI: 10.1145/1394427.1394430 1.3

Sheldon, Nathan, Eric Girard, Seth Borg, Mark Claypool, and Emmanuel Agu. 2003. "The Effect of Latency on User Performance in Warcraft III." Pp. 3-14 in *Proceedings of the 2nd Workshop on Network and System Support for Games*. New York: ACM. DOI: 10.1145/963900.963901 3.1

Sherif, Muzafer, O.J. Harvey, B. Jack White, William R. Hood, and Carolyn W. Sherif. 1988. *Intergroup Conflict and Cooperation: The Robbers Cave Experiment*. New York: Harper and Row. 9.3

Smith, M. Brewster, Jerome S. Bruner, and Robert W. White. 1956. *Opinions and Personality*. New York, Wiley. 5.3

Stanton, Howard, Kurt W. Back, and Eugene Litwak. 1956. "Role-Playing in Survey Research," *American Journal of Sociology*, 62: 172-176. DOI: 10.1086/221958 6

Stark, Rodney, and William Sims Bainbridge. 1985. *The Future of Religion*. Berkeley: University of California Press. 2.4

Stark, Rodney, and William Sims Bainbridge. 1987. *A Theory of Religion*. New York: Toronto/Lang. 2.4

Steinkuehler, Constance. 2008. "Massively Multiplayer Online Games as an Educational Technology: An Outline for Research," Educational Technology 48(1):10-21. 9.2

Steinkuehler, Constance, and Marjee Chmiel. 2006. "Fostering Scientific Habits of Mind in the Context of Online Play." Pp. 723-729 in *Proceedings of the 7th International Conference on Learning Sciences*. Bloomington, Indiana: International Society of the Learning Sciences. 9.2

Su, Wen-Poh, Binh Pham, and Aster Wardhani. 2007. "Personality and Emotion-Based High-Level Control of Affective Story Characters," *IEEE Transactions on Visualization and Computer Graphics* 13: 281-293. DOI: 10.1109/TVCG.2007.44 5.4

Suznjevic, Mirko, Maja Matijasevic, and Ognjen Dobrijevic. 2008. "Action Specific Massive Multi-player Online Role Playing Games Traffic Analysis: Case Study of *World of Warcraft*." Pp. 106-107 in Proceedings of the 7th ACM SIGCOMM Workshop on Network and System Support for Games. New York: ACM. DOI: 10.1145/1517494.1517519 3.1

Sweetser, Penelope, and Peta Wyeth. 2005. "GameFlow: A Model for Evaluating Player Enjoyment in Games." *Computers in Entertainment*, 3(3). 5.3

Tarng, Pin-Yun, Kuan-Ta Chen, and Polly Huang. 2008. "An Analysis of WoW Players' Game Hours." In Proceedings of the 7th ACM SIGCOMM Workshop on Network and System Support for Games. New York: ACM. DOI: 10.1145/1517494.1517504 8.3

Tørnquist, Ragnar. 2001. *Prophet Without Honour*. www.anarchy-online.com/anarchy/frontend/files/CONTENT/download/ documents/prophet_without_honour.pdf 9.1

Tychsen, Anders. 2006. "Role Playing Games: Comparative Analysis Across Two Media Platforms." Pp. 75-82 in *Proceedings of the 3rd Australasian Conference on Interactive Entertainment*. Perth, Australia: Murdoch University. 4.3

Tychsen, Anders, Michael Hitchens, Thea Brolund, and Manolya Kavakli. 2005. "The Game Master." Pp. 215-222 in *Proceedings of the Second Australasian Conference on Interactive Entertainment*. Sydney, Australia: Creativity and Cognition Studios Press. 4.3

Vallerand, Robert J., Céline Blanchard, Geneviève A. Mageau, Richard Koestner, Catherine Ratelle, Maude Léonard, Marylène Gagné, and Josée Marsolais. 2003. "Les Passions de l'Âme: On Obsessive and Harmonious Passion," *Journal of Personality and Social Psychology*, 85:756–767. DOI: 10.1037/0022-3514.85.4.756 5.3

Von Neumann, John, and Oskar Morgenstern. 1944. *Theory of Games and Economic Behavior*. Princeton, New Jersey: Princeton University Press. 9

Walther, Bo Kampmann. 2005. "Atomic Actions - Molecular Experience: Theory of Pervasive Gaming." *Computers in Entertainment* 3(3). 1.1

Wang, Chih-Chien, and Yi-Shiu Chu. 2007. "Harmonious Passion and Obsessive Passion in Playing Online Games," *Social Behavior and Personality*, 35:997-1006. DOI: 10.2224/sbp.2007.35.7.997 5.3

Webb, Steven Daniel, and Sieteng Soh. 2007. "Cheating in Networked Computer Games: A Review." Pp. 105-112 in *Proceedings of the 2nd International Conference on Digital Interactive Media in Entertainment and Arts*. New York: ACM. DOI: 10.1145/1306813.1306839 4.2

Whitney-Robinson, Voronica. 2004. *Star Wars Galaxies: The Ruins of Dantooine*. New York: Ballantine. 9.1

Williams, Dmitri. 2006. "Virtual Cultivation: Online Worlds, Offline Perceptions," *Journal of Communications* 56:69-87. DOI: 10.1111/j.1460-2466.2006.00004.x 9.3

Williams, Dmitri, Nicolas Duchenaut, Li Xiong, Yuanyuan Zhang, Nick Yee, and Eric Nickell. 2006. "From Tree House to Barracks: The Social Life of Guilds in World of Warcraft," *Games and Culture* 1: 338-361. DOI: 10.1177/1555412006292616 8.3

Winnicott, D.W. 1971. *Playing and Reality*. New York: Basic Books. 9

Yang, Kuo-shu, and Michael Harris Bond. 1990. "Exploring Implicit Personality Theories with Indigenous or Imported Constructs: The Chinese Case," *Journal of Personality and Social Psychology* 58: 1087-1095. DOI: 10.1037/0022-3514.58.6.1087 5.1

Yee, Nick. 2006. "The Demographics, Motivations and Derived Experiences of Users of Massively-Multiuser Online Graphical Environments." *PRESENCE: Teleoperators and Virtual Environments* 15: 309-329. DOI: 10.1162/pres.15.3.309 5.2

Yee, Nick. 2009. "Befriending Ogres and Wood-Elves: Relationship Formation and The Social Architecture of Norrath." *Game Studies* 9(1); http://gamestudies.org/0901/articles/yee 5.2

Zeisel, Hans. 1982a. "Disagreement over the Evaluation of a Controlled Experiment," *American Journal of Sociology* 88:378-389. DOI: 10.1086/227676 9.3

Zeisel, Hans. 1982b. "Hans Zeisel Concludes the Debate," *American Journal of Sociology* 88:394-396. DOI: 10.1086/227678 9.3

Author's Biography

WILLIAM SIMS BAINBRIDGE

William Sims Bainbridge is the author of 18 books and about 200 articles in the areas of sociology of technology, social movements, and research methodologies. For his recent book, God from the Machine, he programmed a neural network multi-agent system to simulate religious cognition and conversion in a large community. His book about World of Warcraft, The Warcraft Civilization, has recently been published by MIT Press. After organizing the first large scientific meeting inside World of Warcraft in May 2008, he edited a book growing out of the proceedings, Online Worlds, published by Springer. He spends well over a thousand hours each year doing observational research inside virtual worlds, and he is currently writing a pair of books on how gameworlds explore both the future and the past of humanity. For the last seventeen years, he has served as a program officer managing review of grant proposals in the social science and computer science directorates of the National Science Foundation. He has extensive experience editing publications on the societal implications of nanotechnology, converging technologies, and human-computer interaction.

Printed in the United States
by Baker & Taylor Publisher Services